AWAKENING

AWAKENING

BY ANURAG SHANTAM

悟り

Rebel Satori Press
Bar Harbor, Maine

Published in the United States of America by
REBEL SATORI PRESS
P.O. Box 363
Hulls Cove, ME 04644
www.rebelsatori.com

Designed by Sven Davisson

ISBN: 978-1-60864-006-5

Library of Congress Cataloging-in-Publication Data

Shantam, Anurag.
 Awakening / by Anurag Shantam.
    p. cm.
 ISBN 978-1-60864-006-5 (pbk.)
 1. Spirituality. 2. God. 3. Transcendence (Philosophy)
 I. Title.
 BL624.S4769 2009
 204'.4--dc22
                          2009032932

Contents

Introduction	1
1. Beginnings	5
2. Who Are You?	7
3. The Ego	13
4. The Concept of Trinity	25
5. The Veils	31
6. The Spirit Center	35
7. The Soul Center	45
8. The God Center	63
9. Passing Through the Veils	77
10. Meditations	109
11. The Journey Home	115
12. Sex	143
Centers of Consciousness	152
The Prism Diagram	158
Conclusion	161
Illustrations	
Centers of Consciousness	151
The Prism Diagram	157

Introduction

For many it appears to be the end times. Whether the world is about to end or not remains to be seen. What does appear certain is that we are teetering on the brink of catastrophe. Whether terrorists succeed in destabilizing governments and plunging the world into chaos and a new dark age, or the continuing assault on the environment results in the collapse of the web

The collective soul of mankind is in more peril today than at any time in history.

of life, the future looks anything but bright. Everywhere we look, governments, social institutions and corporations seem corrupt beyond redemption. Contracts between people and the institutions serving them, once based on trust, have been replaced with fear, suspicion and anger. The social fabric is torn by acrimony and blame, and genocide continues to show its ugly face across the globe. The violence we saw delivered by large armies in the 20th century can now, in the 21st century, be delivered by individuals. A single person with a weapon of mass destruction can set the world ablaze.

The problems facing us are so monumental that they seem unsolvable, even though they are manmade. While we are collectively destroying our lives, our children's lives, and life itself, we feel powerless in the face of the complexity of our dilemma to do anything about it, save to scramble to secure our piece of the pie. The collective soul of mankind is in more peril today than at any time in history. Experience has shown that neither political action nor education has been effective in eliminating suffering, and now we are in a spiritual crisis that will not be solved by politicians, educators, social scientists, or well-meaning religious leaders.

But we are not powerless to avert the looming disasters confronting us. In fact, we are the *only* ones who can begin to change the nightmare that life has become. This is so because we are, individual by individual by individual, its very cause.

What I propose with this book may seem radical to some, simplistic to others. But we are in the endgame, and only a radical shift in consciousness will help us avert disaster. This shift will not begin at the top, with the institutions that govern and direct our lives, and move down to each of you. It will instead begin with each of you, and move upwards to the institutions that we create. It seems that only a miracle could save the world now, and that is the point of this book—to ignite and provoke each of you to create a miracle.

The concepts that I introduce here will guide you through the process of awakening—the process that collectively can make the miracle real. These concepts are pointers to transcendence, to *one*-ness, to paradise—to enlightenment. Although the West has had its share of enlightened beings, the West has no tradition of enlightenment. The few awakened beings we know of have been turned into Gods with super powers, resulting in religions that enslave rather than liberate, and hold worshippers in a perpetual state of unworthiness. In the East, enlightenment has always been the goal, always recognizable as potentially attainable by any being seeking liberation. Enlightenment is misunderstood in the West. Even among those who seek it, few really believe that it exists, or is attainable. Many of those who do believe it exists also believe it is so difficult to attain that it will take multiple lifetimes to achieve.

In truth, each of us is already enlightened. What I teach is not how to attain an exalted state, but rather how to uncover something that exists in every being. I have heard enlightenment referred to as being extraordinarily ordinary. It is.

Throughout the book I use the terms *enlightenment* and *awakening* interchangeably, for they describe the same thing. As you move through the awakening process, you will feel as if you are awakening from a bad dream. This is the light of consciousness withdrawing from the ego darkness. In other words, to awaken is to reclaim your inner light.

1. Beginnings

Like many seeking enlightenment, I felt like a spiritual outsider from an early age. While outwardly accepting the teachings of the church into which I was born, including the concepts of original sin, damnation and redemption, inwardly I was empty and dissatisfied, and in considerable pain. In my adolescence, psychotherapy emerged as the new religion in America. It held the promise of healing—that is, it held the promise of being able to do what the old religion could not. I turned my back on organized religion and studied to become a therapist. For years I also underwent various types of therapy, but nothing seemed to fulfill me spiritually. I could always talk about my fear and pain, but my suffering did not change. I became more adept at masking my emptiness and fitting into the world, but this was never enough. And so I began to explore alternative practices and philosophies.

During my journey I was introduced to the concept of transcendence—that is, not simply talking about fear and pain, but actually transcending to a state that was beyond both. The world of Eastern Mysticism was opening to me, but I was not yet ready to enter it. I continued to explore alternative spiritual practices, but was still deeply attached to my fear and pain. Slowly, I began to realize that my choices were being driven as much by this attachment, as they were by the part of me that was searching. In other words, I wanted to have a spiritual journey to enlightenment, but I wanted a safe journey. I believed I could gain enlightenment by carrying this precious cargo of fear and pain through the gates of Paradise. This cargo was an integral part of my *ego*.

What I did not know then was that in order to become spiritually enlightened, the ego must die. The ego is an illusion, but a powerful one that does not want to die. Therefore, even as I searched for transcendence and enlightenment, I was drawn to teachings that did not threaten the ego. I was drawn to teachings that were safe. Safe in what way? *I won't have to deal with my fear. I can safely talk about my fear in my head, for as long as I do this I don't have to deal with the problem itself. I can talk endlessly about my pain, but I want nothing to interfere with it. For what would happen to me if the pain were dissolved? If my fear and pain are part of me and I kill them, I am killing me.*

The years moved unhappily by. Then in 1980 I met two disciples of a Master whose photograph each of them carried in a locket at the end of a *mala*. I was powerfully drawn to the teachings of this Master, and as the weeks passed I came to understand that it was time for me to begin my spiritual journey in earnest.

2. Who Are You?

In 1981 my search led me to India. There I became a student of self-discovery, a disciple of the ancient spiritual traditions of the sub-continent. At the center of these traditions is a simple principle—that to discover who you are now, you must first discover who you have always been. That is, who were you at the beginning?

One technique by which you are led back to this beginning is an ancient one. You sit before a Master who asks, 'Who are you?' You begin relating the story of your life, in which you appear as both the omniscient narrator and the main character. The Master interrupts, and asks again, 'Who are you?' You take your story in another direction, adding sub-plots, events and more characters. The Master interrupts and asks again, 'Who are you?' Each time you begin, the Master stops you and repeats his question. Eventually, you realize that the story you have been trying very hard to tell is just that ... a *story* about who you are. The power of the Master's question is that it reveals a profound truth. You are not your story. You are, in fact, lost in its narrative.

The power of the Master's question is that it reveals a profound truth. You are not your story. You are, in fact, lost in its narrative.

The Master's technique is similar to that used in Western

psychotherapy, where once again you begin your clinical quest to discover who the *you* is that requires therapy, essentially by relating a story. The therapist helps you peel through the story's many layers to the truth, knowing that as long as you are caught up in the story, you will never discover the person who is lost in the story.

When I returned from India, I set out to discover who this being was who was lost in my own story. I knew that if I could get back to the origin of my story, I could transcend it and discover myself. During this journey I came to understand the origin of not only my own story, but of the story of mankind. This archetypal tale is the paradigm that underlies the process of *Awakening*—the arrival at an Eden-like state of consciousness.

In his discussions of the power of myth, Joseph Campbell points out that there is an original myth that underlies the world's major belief systems. It is the myth of the creation.

In Western tradition, this tale begins and ends with the first three chapters of Genesis. In chapters one and two, God creates the world. He blesses his creation and pronounces it good. In chapter three God creates two children, a son and a daughter, and places them in a garden paradise. Also present in the garden is a mysterious serpent of unknown origin. Everything in the garden is Adam and Eve's, except the Tree of Knowledge of good and evil, the fruit of which is forbidden to them. Knowledge of good and evil is the key to the story, for in Eden there is no good or evil. Creation is one, undivided— creation does not live in a world of good and evil. It lives in a world of 'is-ness'. It is what it is.

Eating fruit from the Tree of Knowledge of good and evil transports you into a world of separation, a world of duality, a world of conflict. It transports you into the war between good and evil that damns mankind to this very day. By eating the fruit, you don't 'know' good and evil, you have knowledge of good and evil, and knowledge is a borrowed belief. This is the distinction between knowing and believing. If I *believe*, then I am always in conflict with non-believers, trying to convert them to believe as I do. If I *know*, then there is no conflict within or without—for *knowing* is not shadowed by doubt, and does not require outside support, affirmation, and confirmation.

Feminists often use the story of the Fall to illustrate the evil patriarchal nature of western religion. It would seem to be so, for where is the mother in the story? Why doesn't she have a role? And what of Eve—why is the only female in Eden portrayed as evil, responsible for the fall of humanity? On the surface it does appear unbalanced, unfair, and patriarchal. However, while the story is often politicized—sometimes to oppress women, sometimes to oppress men—it is a nonpolitical, spiritual tale. If you are going to understand it, penetrate to its sublime depths, you must set aside the politics of good and evil and prepare to delve deeper. And yes, the mother was there—not as a person, but as a symbol. She is the serpent.

The serpent tempts Eve, promising that if she eats the fruit of the Tree of Knowledge, she will become Godlike. Eve eats from the apple, and tempts Adam to do the same. Suddenly they recognize their nakedness—their sexual differences. That is, they recognize that they are different from one another. By eating the apple they step into a world of separation. In the world of good and evil already inhabited by God, they become like God—just as the serpent promised. They have entered the world of duality.

God discovers that his children have eaten the forbidden fruit, and becomes angry. Adam, the son, becomes frightened. Eve, the daughter, is cursed with sorrow. Both are cast out of the garden, and their long journey of suffering begins.

Scripture indicates something else significant about the creation myth. A good and creative God enters the garden, but it is an angry, vengeful, destructive God who leaves it. The remainder of the Bible is a *story*, the story of the interactions and relationships of this father God and his children. In this story all the characters are trying to return to the Eden-like world of the garden.

We can all relate to this story. It is a narrative whose plot elements we plagiarize for use in our own individual stories … love, ambition, hope, war, music, treachery, joy, deception, creation and destruction. The creation myth exists in one form or another across all world religions. It is universal—as universal as the taxing and complicated story of mankind's existence after the fall from grace. This is the myth and subsequent story of every human being.

The Creation story points to a profound truth about who we are—not a factual truth, but a spiritual truth, and to grasp this truth is to unlock the mystery of your individual drama as you navigate through the world of good and evil. The key is to focus on who left the garden—an angry, vengeful, jealous, destructive father God who blames His children for the fall of His creation. He lays down rules that are impossible to obey, then punishes His children for not performing according to His standards. He punishes and seeks to destroy others who do not believe as He does. He is arbitrary and, at times, cruel. There is little if anything lovable about Him, yet He demands love.

This father God is always watching over His children—criticizing and condemning, judging them often and praising them rarely. A daughter, Eve, is the human Soul. She is tender, sensitive and loving. She is cursed by the father with sorrow, and blamed by Him for the fall of paradise. A son, Adam, is the human Spirit. He is fun, adventurous and trusting, but frightened by the father's anger. Feeling like a failure in God's eyes, the son is crippled by fear and insecurity.

Inside each of us is a part that is angry, a part that harbors thoughts of revenge against enemies, is jealous of happiness in others, and wants to control others with hidden lists of rules, of *shoulds*, that we arbitrarily impose. This is our angry God. Inside each of us is a part that is lonely and sorrowful, a part that always feels guilty and responsible for failure—in your own life as well as in the lives

The good, creative, blessing God who entered the garden became the three parts of who we are – the trinity that left the garden.

of others. This is our Soul. Inside of each of us is a part that is frightened and insecure, always seeking approval from others. This is our Spirit. These three parts are the same three parts described in creation scripture. They are lost in individual ego dramas, searching for each other—for the wholeness, the *oneness* they once were. They are futilely searching *out there* for what is hidden right beside them, inside. They are you.

The good, creative, blessing God who entered the garden became the three parts of who we are—the trinity that left the garden. We are the judgmental, controlling father, the hurting guilty daughter, and the insecure frightened son. This is what is hidden inside. This is the mystery the creation story reveals. How this came about—to begin to understand the spiritual dynamic and drama of our interior lives, we must first understand the nature of *ego*.

3. The Ego

The ego. What is it? If you ask ten people, you will most likely receive ten different explanations. Ego pathology, or dysfunction, is endless. There are numerous books describing various ego pathologies, with new pathologies being 'discovered' daily (along with the attendant 'experts' to treat them). Since there is so much confusion around the concept of ego, I will provide you with a simple explanation. You will then have some idea of what I am talking about when I talk about ego. In all likelihood, my explanation will be somewhat different from whatever concepts or beliefs you already hold.

The ego I am speaking of is, very simply, the beliefs, patterns, defenses, memories and bad feelings associated with your sorrow-pain states, your anxiety-fear states, and your anger-bitterness states—in short, everything hidden within that creates for you a life of suffering. The ego *is* your suffering, and when I speak about dissolving the ego, I am speaking about dissolving that suffering.

Because ego is also an illusion, I am also speaking of awakening you from the illusion or dream of suffering. Since something real (you) is lost in the ego illusion of suffering, the suffering too seems very real. But like being lost in a dream that seems real, when you awaken you see that it was not real at all. Awakening from the ego nightmare is a very similar experience, though not as sudden. This awakening happens in stages, as you move through different states of consciousness. As you attain each state, you look back on what preceded it and it looks like a dream. It appears this way because it is.

As you awaken into clarity, you see and *know* that all you experienced prior was essentially a dream—that you were in a dream state, projecting the dream onto reality. You slowly awaken into reality, with more and more of you in the light of *now*, and less and less of you in the ego darkness of the past. Ego cannot exist in the *now*, for it is not real, and *now* is the only reality there is. Ego cannot experience *now*. It is always taking you into either a painful, illusionary past, or a fearful illusionary future. Because the ego is an illusion, it can never experience real states. Love is real. Ego can never know what love is, and therefore can never love. Trust is real. The ego can never know trust. How could something born in fear know trust? Ego's pretense of trust is rooted in fear and expectations of betrayal. Truth is real. Ego can never know truth. Ego can believe any number of crazy contradictory things, but all of its beliefs will be shrouded with doubt that can never be quelled. The ego can never know anything with the certainty that brings peace, and as long as there is ego-created warfare within each of us, there will never be peace in the world.

Lost in the ego nightmare of suffering, we are unaware

> *As you awaken into clarity, you see and know that all you experienced prior was essentially a dream – that you were in a dream state, projecting the dream onto reality.*

that we are creating it. As a result, we do not understand that we have the power to *un*-create it. All you need is a way to un-create it, and the motivation to end this suffering once and for all. However, one of the first realizations of any seeker embarking on the journey of awakening is discovering just how precious our suffering is to us. We ask, *without my suffering, my pain, my fear, my anger, what would be left of me?* What will be left are things you have not known for a long time— unconditional love, unconditional trust, truth, and bliss. These are what have been lost in the ego nightmare of separation, of suffering.

My definition of ego is, therefore: Painful, fearful separation from myself and my world. Angry resentment at the way life has turned out. Conflict, dishonor, disease, lies, deceitfulness, greed, heartlessness, and at the very center of the ego darkness—hatred. To awaken is to part with all of these things, and to become a light in the world.

Ego and the Metaphor of the Wave

A wave arises in the ocean, rides the surface a while, and then abates. Does anyone celebrate its birth or mourn its demise? No. The wave is part of the unique expression of the ocean, which itself seems eternal, never being born or dying. So too, out of the ocean of consciousness arise the myriad forms we see around us. Each form is a unique expression, or wave, in the eternal ocean of consciousness. Each wave arising from the ocean of consciousness assumes a form, a unique expression developed over millions of years of evolution. The wave abates, consciousness returns to the ocean, and the form dies, only to be reborn again with the rise of a new wave. Nothing is actually born or dies, because the consciousness animating these forms is eternal.

With the notable exception of man, life forms are not disconnected from this ocean of consciousness. They are not fighting it, not trying to control it, not expecting it to be turbulent or calm, and not fearing or anticipating death. Most of nature lives in the eternal *now*.

Imagine a wave in the sea, somehow becoming trapped in a container. Trapped, the wave is unable to flow naturally with the sea's currents. In the beginning the container is as transparent as glass, but over time it becomes dirty, and as debris attaches to it, it eventually becomes a rigid structure. As more debris attaches to it, the container becomes more rigid, more dense. Because the wave

The wave believes the hard container is reality, and that everything must be done to strengthen it, for the container is all that protects the wave from the unpredictable ocean threatening it.

inside is no longer able to flow, it loses contact with its very nature. It identifies more and more with the container. It begins to believe it *is* the container, set adrift in an alien and threatening landscape. The wave forgets it is a wave. The wave forgets that it is still part of the ocean around it, believing instead that it is the rigid container whose stability and integrity is threatened by a capricious and unpredictable environment.

Thinking itself the container, believing its existence is dependent on the container, the wave struggles unsuccessfully to strengthen it, and thus control the ocean. Over time though, the wave grows increasingly unhappy. It is unable to flow. It is restrained. But having been in the container for so long, bumping into other containers similarly encrusted with debris, seemingly also adrift in the ocean, the wave has forgotten it was once the ocean. It has forgotten that it once flowed free. The wave's long imprisonment in the container feels so familiar, it believes the dim memories of flow and freedom to be nothing but dreams and illusions.

The wave believes the hard container *is* reality, and that everything must be done to strengthen it, for the container is all that protects the wave from the unpredictable ocean threatening it. Imagine a wave feeling alien to the ocean around it, creating beliefs and myths to justify and explain why the structure imprisoning it exists. Imagine the wave's surprise if the structure containing it were to dissolve, allowing the wave to rejoin the ocean and flow free. Imagine the wave discovering that it was, and still is, the ocean itself—the same ocean the wave had been blaming for feelings of separation, alienation and constant danger.

Such is the fate of man, a wave in the ocean of consciousness, held separate by what at first was a subtle transparent sensation, a subtle separation from the ocean of consciousness, opening a new opportunity for evolution. An opportunity for parts of consciousness to become detached from the ocean, to begin exploring the nature of consciousness itself in the only way possible—by becoming separate from it. The ego veils began just like that, as subtle walls of separation, allowing individual parts of the ocean of consciousness to separate and explore creation and the consciousness creating and sustaining it.

At first it was new and exciting. The veils were thin and transparent, and allowed individual consciousness to explore and dance with creation. It was magic. For a very long time it was magic. The veils made something new possible in creation. The same wave could exist over time, incarnating in one human form after another, enabling deep sustained exploration of the nature of creation and consciousness, and the development of creative gifts that could not be attained in one lifetime alone. Such is the miracle of man. This is why children born to the same parents and growing up in the same environment, turn out so differently. Hidden in each one is a long unique history that even the most pervasive social conditioning cannot entirely destroy. We are not born clear slates for social scientists to fill with the beliefs and *shoulds* of our culture. The slate we carry into this life contains the writings of many lifetimes, a sort of spiritual pentimento. Each new human is uniquely drawn to different areas of interest, as though each has a natural familiarity or aptitude in that area.

This new evolutionary leap that was the birth of man, of individual consciousness, carried an inevitable flaw. This flaw was neither foreseen nor planned. It just happened. The veils opened a new chapter in evolution, enabling a single part of consciousness to move again and again into human form. But just like the container of the wave, over time the container of consciousness, the veils, became dirty, encrusted, hard and rigid. For with each lifetime, a layer was added to the veils. Over time, the consciousness that is *you* began to experience more and more separation from the world of which you are obviously a part. As the veils thickened, the sense of *you* was replaced with a sense of the veils. You began to identify with the veils, which resulted in an increasing feeling of separation. You felt the *thing* which held you separate, but you mistakenly thought of it as being you.

With the growth of the veils and mankind's growing identification with them, the light of consciousness was dimmed. For many beings, it became very dark indeed. The veils assumed labels and identities, and because they are shared by all human beings, they were assumed to be a natural human component. The veils seemed to be a given, an unalterable condition. Though they did not feel good, they did feel familiar. From the speculation of why the suffering produced by these veils existed, arose all of the philosophies and religions that continue to this day.

The reason these philosophies and religions have all failed to answer the essential questions facing humanity is that they are all based on a false premise. That is, that the veils and all the confusion and suffering produced by them, are an unalterable component of being human. They are not. The veils are simply the accumulated dirt covering the lenses through which you look into the world, distorting all you see, interpreting reality as the distortion. Each life adds another layer to the veils. Each successive life experienced as being sadder, more disconnected, scarier, and angrier at the seeming unfairness and meaninglessness of it all.

In truth, you suffer because you are creating your life through the ego veils of suffering. Dissolve the veils and you dissolve suffering. Life goes on with its challenges, its highs and lows. The only difference will be that you do not suffer and feel a helpless victim. Life becomes what it is—no longer a struggle, no longer a war—simply a unique wave, moving in the great ocean of life. Earth is not a penal colony. We are not here to suffer for past transgressions, or to

In truth, you suffer because you are creating your life through the ego veils of suffering. Dissolve the veils and you dissolve suffering.

learn lessons. This is not the reform school the ego claims. It is simply life. It is what it is, an un-foldment of consciousness, with no meaning and no grand design. It is more like an exploration of limitless potential. You are the explorer and the potential, you are the seeker and the sought.

Older souls seem to carry a heaviness produced by the thickening of veils over countless lifetimes. At times they seem jaded, as though they have seen it all before, and know it is much ado about nothing. They will seem less excited about life, less enthralled at the ego distractions of the world. For indeed they have seen it all countless times before. When such souls awaken, they contain a storehouse of wisdom. But such wisdom can only be released through lifting of the veils. Younger souls tend to be more drawn into the world, more excited by the world's possibilities. To them, the world and its experiences are still new and unexplored. They tend to have a lightness, an adventurousness lacking in older souls, who tend to seek peace, rest, and an end to the journey.

But the call to awaken goes out to young and old souls alike. A cycle of darkness is coming to its inevitable conclusion. We must each awaken, renew the earth, and ignite a new glorious cycle. If we do not, the world will die. It will no longer be a place for consciousness to evolve, to reach new heights. The fate of the world rests with you.

Ego and a Metaphor of Science

In the scientific quest, we have been taught that the brain is synonymous with consciousness—that the brain is the seat of consciousness. This is understandable only because science is limited to the exploration of the physical world. No matter how sophisticated or penetrating science becomes, it can never go *beyond* the physical manifestation of consciousness to explore consciousness itself. To enter and explore consciousness, one must enter through the gate of the human Soul, and the Soul is something that science denies exists. Despite the fact that Soul cannot be proven logically, rationally or scientifically, one can *know* its existence even in ego sleep. Consciousness too can be known, but not proven scientifically.

> *To enter and explore consciousness, one must enter through the gate of the human Soul, and the Soul is something that science denies exists.*

The brain seems to be the center of consciousness because we are always living there, in its constant flow of mindless, repetitive chatter. The brain is a bio-computer, used by your consciousness to process information as you move through, and interact with, the world. When you are in ego darkness, your brain becomes a false center of consciousness. The bio-computer which is meant to be used by you, becomes your master. It becomes a very powerful instrument controlled by something false, claiming to be you. In the material world, an electronic computer functions very much like the ego controlled bio-computer. It promises freedom, but delivers slavery. It stores and links information, but cannot know. It allows access to an unlimited volume of

Once awakened, your brain begins to function as it was intended, as an instrument to enable consciousness to process information that is received through the senses.

contradictory and confusing facts, but cannot itself make sense of them. Like its biological counterpart, the brain, the electronic computer too is plagued by pop-ups, advertising jingles and images, and intrusions of other people forcing their information on us—all of it unwanted and unasked for.

Just as the ego controlled brain promises freedom and fulfillment and fails to deliver either one, so too the electronic computer further enslaves us, by virtue of the egos that have designed it and those who use it. Like all creations in the world of good and evil, the electronic computer delivers both.

Once awakened, your brain begins to function as it was intended, as an instrument to enable consciousness to process information that is received through the senses. You begin to use this instrument, rather than be used by it. In the process of awakening, you will also discover moments when the internal bio-computer seems to stop—as if not being needed, it simply shuts down. These moments allow you to experience what the ego abhors, which is silence. And in that silence you experience the beginning of something you have probably not known since childhood—and that is peace.

In that silence, with no thoughts or commercials or *shoulds*, you begin to realize that to be conscious does not require the constant noise being generated in the brain by the ego. In that silence you begin to understand that consciousness is separate from the brain—that it permeates the whole body—and that the brain, far from being the center of consciousness is, like a computer, a powerful instrument that you can use when necessary and turn off when it is just a noisy distraction.

Science can manipulate brain chemistry to alter moods, creating a desensitized and overmedicated nation. Mood altering drugs are nothing new, but like all drugs, over time they lose their effectiveness, and require ever increasing dosages or newer and more powerful formulas. While they may alter moods by altering chemistry, they cannot touch the underlying consciousness that is causing the imbalanced chemistry in the first place. When you stop taking these drugs, you return to your previous troubled state, if not to a worse state, for the chemicals themselves will effect further and unforeseen imbalances.

Transform consciousness, and brain chemistry will change on its own. Eliminate the ego imbalance in consciousness, and the physical vehicle of consciousness will change as well—permanently. The similarity between the electronic and the biological computer which created it, is summed up by the programmer adage—*garbage in, garbage out*. Like its electronic counterpart, the brain has been stuffed with other peoples garbage, which it constantly regurgitates, driving you mad.

4. The Concept of Trinity

We think of ourselves as a unity. There is one of us. But we are, in fact, engaged in an unending and often unpleasant internal dialogue of conflicting opinions. We condemn and praise ourselves, but if we are a single entity, how can we be in conflict with ourselves? In order to have conflict, there must be at least two players. When I am condemning myself, part of me is pointing a finger and feeling powerful, and another part is receiving the condemnation and feeling bad. Though on the deepest level, we *are* each a unity, we are not living in that unity consciousness. We live instead in a state of divided, split consciousness. In such a state, we are in conflict with ourselves. If you are in conflict with yourself, the only certainty is that you will lose every single time. Therefore, to heal conflict and bring the divided consciousness back into one, you must first understand something of the nature of human consciousness, and the concept of *trinity*.

The difference between man and lower life forms is that unlike the latter, humans are capable of observing themselves—of being conscious of themselves. When I am sad, I am also aware of my sadness. In other words, part of me is sad, but another part of me observes my sadness and may even comment on it or attempt to change it. Whatever state I may be experiencing, another part of me has the ability to step outside of myself to observe. If I had a unified consciousness, I would be in total sadness, without any awareness detached from and aware of the sadness, and with no way to consciously change my state. Does this mean there are only two centers of consciousness, one that experiences and one that observes? Or are there more than two?

Though the concept of trinity exists in other religions, in Christianity it is expressed as the Holy Trinity of the Father, Son and Holy Ghost. There is a judgmental father, or God, inside each of us. He is resentful at the way life has turned out for you individually, and the way it has turned out for mankind collectively. There is a son, or Spirit. He is very insecure, constantly feeling he is not good enough, not smart enough, not productive enough, doesn't work hard enough ... a son who never seems to live up to the expectations of others or of the father. There is a daughter, a Soul. The Soul inside us is our love center—it is from our Soul that we love, seek love, seek connection. When we experience moments of extreme tenderness—that is when we're touching our Soul. This is a most difficult period in history for the Soul, one in which she is valued very little. In many ways, modern society is basically anti-Soul. In western tradition, the spirit of regeneration, the Holy Ghost, is the Soul.

Each of the three parts, or centers of consciousness—Spirit, Soul, and God—has its own desires, needs and aspirations. In religion and psychology, each can be further divided into different personalities, or archetypes, but it is with the three elemental centers themselves that we will concern ourselves.

Before we examine these three centers, let us return for a moment to the events in the garden and revisit not only God's own transformation, but also the effect of His transformation on our own stories.

We accept that human beings are the fallen children, fated to experience suffering in the vale of tears. We believe that God is watching us from some divine 'out there', totting up the score and judging our individual performances. Yet, the most significant piece of the myth is often overlooked. Though we understand the misfortune of Adam and Eve, we overlook the fact that God too fell. Not only did the children of God leave the garden—He left with them. They all fell from grace. With the events of Eden, He changed from being the creative, good and blessing God who entered the garden, into the angry, vengeful, destructive God who left it. Within a few chapters of mankind's story, we hear of God creating genocide against all life on earth to punish His fallen children.

To heal conflict and bring the divided consciousness back into one, you must first understand that parts of the internal trinity are in conflict.

Is God really doing this from on high? Or rather, if we are made in His image, is he doing it through us? Inside of every human being there is an angry vengeful God keeping track of all deeds. He is experienced as the internal judge, the part that seeks to control life, both within and without. He's the part that likes to be in control. He is that perfectionist inside, and we cannot live up to His idea of perfection. He cannot even do that.

Even though the creator of this world is inside of every one of us, His creativity has been transformed into creative destruction. In each one of us, this great God of creation has the ability to destroy His very creation. In the garden, He blamed Adam and Eve for the destruction of Paradise, the beginning of the "blame game" which continues unabated to this day. This destructive finger pointing is destroying our own world. Each one of us is unwittingly participating in this destruction. You are the Father who is judging and blaming, overseeing life. You are the son, who is anxious and afraid. You are the daughter, the guilty, sorrowful soul. You are all of them.

Nevertheless, you do not believe you are all of them. Each of our individual Gods believes He is on the side of good. Our individual Gods want to be good, but our concepts of good and evil are an accident of birth. Our belief systems are rooted in the cultures and political systems, the societies and families into which we are born. We do not *know* that something is good or evil—we *believe* it is good or evil. Our individual Gods have beliefs that divide the world into good and evil. In this state, God is in a place of belief—and wherever there is belief, there is a shadow of doubt behind it.

Each individual God tries to find and join other individual Gods with similar beliefs, for doing so strengthens the belief system. Each also rejects the individual Gods that do not adhere to the belief system, forming an impenetrable barrier of anger. When an individual God is *Awakened*, He not only slips out of the divided world of good and evil—He slips from a place of *belief* into a place of *knowing*. He then knows certain things are true, but no longer needs others to verify the truth—at that point truth is self-evident. An *Awakened* God is one who has slipped out of the divided world of good and evil and become available to listen to other Gods and their truths.

The creative and blessing God who is in all of us must be awakened from this nightmare that He and we are caught in. We must individually awaken Him within us. If we do not, He will continue to destroy His creation. My goal is to point the way home by *Awakening* this God in all of us, and inevitably answer the Master's question, 'Who are you?'

5. The Veils

Before exploring the nature of the three centers of consciousness, we must first introduce those things that hold the Spirit, Soul and God centers from each other. These are the *veils of separation*. Each center within you looks into the world through a different veil. The veil determines what you see, and how you interpret your experiences. This is where we enter the ego experience of separation. The veils are the roots of the ego illusion. As such, they are the most fiercely defended part of the ego structure. Think of the ego as a parasitic plant attached to your tree of life. It siphons off your strength, aliveness, and as it grows, denies you the light and recognition of existence, leaving you feeling that no one sees you. You are correct. You are veiled by an alien ego growth pretending to be you. Therapy can help prune the ego growth to make you more functional and socially acceptable, but the ego continues to grow—nourished by event patterns established in childhood. This alien is full of hot buttons and boundaries, all linked to and protecting its roots—the veils. The veils are the place where the ego attaches to you and feeds off your centers of consciousness, denying you life and fulfillment.

Before exploring the Spirit, Soul and God centers in depth, let us look at the relationship of the veils to each of the three.

The first center of consciousness is Spirit. It is located in the solar plexus, where you experience what is called your 'gut feelings'. The center of human Spirit is masculine. The veil that surrounds and cripples the human Spirit is the *veil of fear*. When you are in a fearful state, you are in your Spirit center looking at the world through fear. This fear distorts reality. In such a state you react to an illusion that your fear has projected onto reality. You give the fear your power, and in return, the fear promises to keep you safe. Herein lies the deception of the ego illusion. Fear is telling you, Spirit, that you need it to keep you safe. This seems logical, but it is not. By asking

The veil that surrounds and cripples the human Spirit is the veil of fear.

yourself a simple question, you will discover the fallacy. When you are caught in the fear, do you feel most safe or most unsafe? How often has fear told you something that in the end turned out to be a lie? And you, Spirit, do you really need fear to tell you when there is danger? If you can understand how often your fear has been wrongly placed, it would be obvious that however flawed your perception might be, reality cannot be worse than the lies perpetuated by your own fear.

The second center of consciousness is Soul. It is located in the area of the heart. The Soul center is feminine—the seat of love and intuition. Our perception through this center is neither logical nor rational. From our Soul center comes a longing to feel whole—to find a Soul mate. The Soul frequently believes she *has* found him, only to see her hopes dashed. She will never feel complete until she is freed from this quest to find a mate. Unknown to her, her true Soul mate, Spirit, is hidden right beside her. All Soul mates outside are at best imperfections of the perfection hidden within. Of all the centers, the descent of the Soul into the darkness of the ego illusion is the most tragic, for she is helpless. When you feel helpless, you are in your Soul center. The ego distortion of the

The veil that surrounds and tortures the human Soul is the veil of pain.

Soul's light illuminates the hopeless romantic. Without the ego, Soul is neither hopeless nor romantic. She simply is. The veil that surrounds and tortures the human Soul is the *veil of pain*. The veils separate us from the world—but for the Soul this is especially onerous, as it is her very nature to connect.

The third center of consciousness is God. Its physical location is the third eye, and its essence is truth. God is masculine. Because God contains all potentiality, when you feel powerful you are in your God center. You are not held back by fear, which is Spirit's problem. Spirit is not there. You are

God is hidden behind and blinded by His own veil – the veil of anger.

not held back by concerns about hurting someone. This is Soul's problem, and Soul is not there. Only God is there, constrained by neither fear nor pain. The tragedy of this God is that his essence is good, truthful and perfect, but He finds himself possessed by evil—forced to perpetrate ugliness that He invariably regrets later on. He longs to be looked up to, to be respected and loved. But He is not, for He is hidden behind and blinded by His own veil—the *veil of anger*. All He sees is what the angry ego shows Him. All He wants to do is what the angry ego is urging Him to do. Made deaf as well by the anger veil, He is unable to hear what anyone is saying to Him. All He hears are the words of the angry ego illusion.

Inside of each of us is both the most obvious place and yet the last place where anyone would look for an angry God, for who wants to be the home of such a being? Nevertheless, He is indeed in each of us—in six billion beings—all of whom are angry, blaming, and destroying the world.

6. The Spirit Center

The Spirit center is located in the *solar plexus*. When you experience a 'gut reaction' that is your Spirit center reacting. The ego veil of darkness surrounding Spirit is fear. When you are anxious or fearful, if you are able to disengage from the fearful thoughts long enough, you will feel an uncomfortable sensation in the area of your stomach. What you are feeling is the veil. More accurately, you are feeling the physical manifestation of Spirit's light being transformed into darkness.

Spirit is inherently perfect. His essence, his spiritual quality, is trust. He unconditionally trusts the fear to protect him. While Soul is intuitive and illogical, Spirit prides himself on his logic and rationality. But when he is gripped by the ego veil of fear, his logic and rationality are the first casualties. The essential deception of ego fear—its message to Spirit—is that Spirit needs the fear to keep him safe. The fallacy of this ego deception is easily revealed by the simple question: *If I need the fear to protect me and keep me safe, why do I feel the most unsafe of all when I am in it?* How many times has ego fear removed you from what, in objective reality, is a perfectly safe environment, and transported you into an internal nightmare?

Just as over time the loving Soul establishes an unhealthy relationship with the pain veil, Spirit does the same with the fear veil. The fear veil becomes his most trusted companion.

Just as the Soul veil doesn't really want her to love anyone but the pain, the fear veil doesn't allow Spirit to trust anyone. The fear veil cannot exist other than by consuming Spirit's light, which he unwittingly, unconditionally with his innocent trust, keeps fueling and sustaining.

The incalculable damage that fear does to you, to your relationship with self, is revealed by these simple questions: *Do you fear love?* That is, do you fear your Soul? *Do you fear truth?* That is, do you fear your God? Remember, the veils transform pure energy into something toxic and destructive. Thoughts generated by the veils, direct the toxic energy. For example—if you fear love, you are inundating your own soul with toxicity. You are lost in the fear veil, directing the fear energy at your Soul, and this looks rational and logical to Spirit.

So who exactly is this Spirit inside of you? He is the part of you that as a child trusted, was fascinated by, and wanted to be a part of the material world in a significant, meaningful way. He is the part who used to be idealistic, who used to believe in the concepts of truth, loyalty, honor, democracy, and more. Spirit received his rude awakening when he was initiated into the ego world of greed, lies, deception and the corruption of everything he formerly trusted. But I am not being entirely accurate when I use the phrase 'formerly trusted'. You see, the Spirit is the seat of unconditional trust. But as the ego veil of fear grew around him, it consumed his light and his trust, transforming it into the opposite—fear and mistrust of everything and everyone.

Spirit wants meaningful work in the world. He wants to take his place in creation and contribute in a meaningful way to his world. He seeks to create structure—home, business, job. Since his reality is the objective world around him, the creation of structure in that world is important to him. In his ego sleep, the deeper significance of need to structure, eludes him—that it is his job to provide a suitable structure to support the passage of the human Soul through this world of matter. But shackled by fear, Spirit never feels safe, and his natural impulse to provide structure becomes distorted into accumulating more things and services, in order to insure safety and keep the fear at bay. Those with monetary wealth know that you cannot purchase security. Unless cleared, the fear veil will continue to make Spirit feel insecure, even in the midst of obvious safety.

> *When you are in your Spirit center, surrounded by a veil of fear, you are still in a state of unconditional trust, but now you are unconditionally trusting the fear.*

Let us approach this from a different direction. When you are in your Spirit center, surrounded by a veil of fear, you are still in a state of unconditional trust, but now you are unconditionally trusting the fear. That is, you are in a state of trusting the very thing that prevents you from trusting anyone outside of you. This fear won't even allow you to trust yourself. The ego structures and lifelong patterns growing out of your fear defends and justifies it, offering explanations for why fear is necessary. You are so sublimated by it that it all seems logical. Fear appears to be a defense that is protecting you.

But if you look more closely, you will see that it is protecting itself—the ego illusion is defending its roots, the only place it is vulnerable.

You must be clear that the fear is not your friend, and it is not serving you. Reflect on what happens when fear grips you—takes you into your head, where over and over again, it plays the same fearful tapes it has played all your life. You have heard them a million times. *I'm not good enough, rich enough, powerful enough, good-looking enough,* ad infinitum.

If the solution to fear could truly be found in the tapes, you would have solved your problems long ago. These fear tapes are familiar, but they are nothing but distractions. They run on the energy of your Spirit and cause you to spin your wheels. When you are in fear, something real is happening, but you do not see reality because the tapes in your head are distracting you with fearful thoughts. You must get out of your head and into reality.

There are two watchers inside everyone. These watchers are referred to as the Witnesses. Spirit is one of the watchers. God is the other. By 'watcher' I mean a certain quality of the masculine centers, the quality of detachment. You might have noticed yourself, maybe at party, slipping into a place of detachment where you find yourself not participating, but simply observing what is happening around you. You are physically present, but detached, observing, witnessing. You are in Spirit or in God, detached and simply watching. Soul cannot do this, for her nature is opposite. Her nature is feminine and connecting.

In order to clear the veils, you *must* cultivate the watcher, for this quality of detachment enables you to sever the flow of light to the veils, thereby dissolving them. Naturally, God is the more powerful watcher, but you cannot count on him—he may be too distracted by his anger to understand, much less begin, the journey home. Spirit can initiate the journey home anytime after you have had enough of being fearful and insecure. When you are sick of the crippled state that fear produces, you can get out of your fearful thoughts and into reality (an uncomfortable sensation) and simply watch. In that perfect detachment you are neither for nor against—and the adventure will begin.

Spirit abhors boredom, and there is no greater adventure than the exploration of the inner world that is called the journey home. Unlike activities in the material world, which offer little satisfaction or sense of accomplishment, the journey home, while having difficulties, rewards Spirit with a sense of meaningful accomplishment. Whether through selfish motivation, to save your Spirit / Soul, or altruistic, to save the world ... whatever your motivation, both goals will be fulfilled simultaneously, and you will have laid the groundwork for the awakening of God.

The Spirit center is the center from which friendship springs—not the deep intimate friendship that is Soul's domain, but 'buddy' or 'girlfriend' type friendship. These are the types of relationships where you enjoy someone's company, but prefer to keep joint activities light and playful. Spirit values his freedom and independence, and prefers to keep his relationships as free of serious entanglements as possible. Someone with a healthy

Spirit center tends to be optimistic, playful, adventurous … at times mischievous in a playful, as opposed to a hurtful, way.

In sexual relationships, Spirit is the part of you that likes to experiment, try new positions, make sex playful and fun. Spirit abhors boredom, as it is his nature to be inquisitive about life. He wants to explore and experience as much as possible. Where Soul is a homebody, Spirit has wanderlust. He is usually the athlete inside, who enjoys team sports that he can participate in with buddies. However, there are areas where the two masculine centers—God and Spirit—overlap, and team sports is one of those areas. Nevertheless, it is easy to distinguish which part is involved. Is the emphasis on teamwork and fun? If so, you are in your Spirit center. Or is the emphasis on competition, destroying the opponent at all cost? If this is the case, you are in your God center. Many athletic activities that used to be fun to Spirit have now been taken over by Gods. With the resulting anger and emphasis on money, enjoyment and fun disappears.

Spirit is the loyal and dedicated worker inside. In the past, his loyalty and dedication were rewarded with praise, perks and security. All that seems to have vanished—for in today's work

Spirit, far from being valued as in the past, has become, like Soul, just another commodity to be purchased, used and discarded.

environments, there is little sense of accomplishement, little satisfaction in a job well done, and any sense of security is rapidly evaportating. To Spirit, work has become meaningless at best, punishing at worst. Spirit, far from being valued as in the past, has become, like Soul, just another commodity to be purchased, used and discarded. Most work environments today are Soul and Spirit deadening, destroyed by ego's heartless focus on efficiency and the bottom line. What keeps Spirit tied to his job is not an innate sense of accomplishment, but the veil of fear.

Spirit is the part of us that likes video and computer games—the active part. Soul likes the passive experience of television, and God is a student of news and politics. Soul and Spirit eschew such serious topics. After all, they think, I have no control and it just scares me (Spirit) or hurts me (Soul). One can clearly see the fallen God in action by watching political talk shows, where angry individual Gods shout at each other. Blinded by their own ideology, they cannot see any other point of view. Each God fights to impose His own truth upon all others.

Spirit is at times a people pleaser, the conciliator inside. Spirit believes in democracy, in talking things out and listening to other points of view. Sometimes this is done out of Spirit's inherent sense of fairness. More often, it is done to diffuse a situation that risks the emergence of some angry God. For in the ego state, Spirit fears God, who continues to terrify Spirit with His blind anger—dominating and controlling Spirit through fear.

Spirit is always seeking God's approval, whether in parents, teachers, boss, friend or beloved. He is always seeking praise and affirmation from the God in others, even as he is doing so with his inner God. Unfortunately, as the ego darkness increases, God's praise and affirmation is replaced by punishment. Spirit perceives this as 'dammed if do, damned if I don't'. This is a correct perception, for God is damning and even if Spirit did everything perfectly and impeccably, he would still find himself damned.

Yet Spirit cannot help, consciously or unconsciously, trying to please God, for Spirit is seeking home. He is trying to heal the split with his inner God in order to become whole again. Unfortunately, the fear veil directs Spirit's attention outward. He seeks to propitiate the Gods of others, when the only God who matters, the only one who can really affirm Spirit, is the God within. Ironically, it takes only a fraction of the energy he wastes on external Gods, to heal the inner dysfunctional family forever—to awaken, and restore Eden.

Since Spirit is also the adventurer inside, I would like to invite him on an adventure to end all adventures. Once having completed it, all others will pale in comparison. This adventure will cost nothing, unlike marketed adventures promoted by the travel industry. You won't have to give anything up,

This adventure is a quest that has a shining prince (Spirit) and an innocent beautiful princess who must to be rescued (Soul).

though much baggage will be willingly discarded on this adventure. Unlike the pseudo adventures marketed by the ego, this adventure will at times be edgy—seeming to push the envelope—and will have challenges, victories and defeats. It will be an adventure cosmic in scale, but at the same time very human and ordinary. It will have extraordinary highs and extraordinary lows. Nothing need outwardly change in your life, though life being what it is, change is inevitable.

This adventure is a quest that has a shining prince (Spirit) and an innocent beautiful princess who must to be rescued (Soul). The prince faces challenges that he overcomes with effort and perseverance, and after overcoming each one he is rewarded with increased powers to help him overcome obstacles ahead. The outcome of this great quest is assured, but Spirit won't know until the end that his success was inevitable from the start. A Master once said of this adventure, "Best not to begin. Once begun, best to finish it." A curious invitation indeed—one that may cause Spirit to tremble as he begins his adventure, but will bring a knowing smile to his lips upon its completion. When I say completion, I mean of course the end of one adventure, and the beginning of another.

At the end of the quest, which has been full of struggle, honor, dedication to an ideal, and the rescue of an innocent maiden from evil—what happens next? The adventure I refer to is the adventure within—the quest of Spirit, who overcomes his fear in order to rescue Soul from her painful imprisonment. Storytellers tell us that in the fairytale the prince and his princess live happily ever after. I echo these words. Spirit and Soul will also live happily ever after.

7. The Soul Center

The Soul center, which is located in the area of the heart, is feminine. Her essence is love. Whether or not you believe in her, everyone has a Soul, for you cannot exist—you cannot anchor in your physical body—without her. She is like the roots of a tree, mysterious and hidden, from which we obtain nourishment. Just as the strength and height of a tree is directly related to its roots, our place in the material world—our individual expressions of Spirit and God in the world—are directly related to strength of our Soul.

The human Soul is also the most delicate, sensitive place within us, a feminine center that men have been taught to fear and despise because she is weak, sensitive, tender, loving and compassionate. Men have been taught to keep their Souls hidden

> *The human Soul is the most delicate, sensitive place within us, a feminine center that men have been taught to fear and despise because she is weak, sensitive, tender, loving and compassionate.*

in order to be safe in the world. Women used to be taught to embrace Soul—to be shy, weak, helpless, loving and caring. Spirit, representing freedom and independence, was denied to women.

With the growing emphasis at the end of the twentieth century on liberating gender, masculine Spirit and masculine God began to be affirmed in women as they had always been in men. Male qualities of competitiveness and aggression took the place of love and family as desirable feminine qualities. While it is empowering for a woman to embrace her masculine centers, she does so at the same terrible price as a man—loss of Soul. A man in denial of his feminine essence is lamentable, but a woman who denies her feminine center to embrace her masculine centers is unimaginable. For the human Soul feels the more natural comfortable center for the female, even as the Spirit center feels the more comfortable natural setting for the male.

Those who are out of touch with their feminine center lack a moral compass. These are the people whose souls are compromised by ego nightmare, their Soul's light completely consumed by the darkness of the pain veil. Where there was feeling and sensitivity, there is now emptiness and deadness. As long as love's light is consumed by the pain veil, we are unable to love. Not incapable of loving, but unable to love—to feel the world around us.

Soul is the first center from which we experience life. Our early years are primarily Soul years—the years not entirely lost in ego darkness—when one can still see her light before it begins to disappear into the ego-darkness and the veil of pain. In these early years one can observe in infants' eyes the innocence and the unconditional

Soul is the first center from which we experience life. Our early years are primarily Soul years – the years not entirely lost in ego darkness – when one can still see her light before it begins to disappear into the ego-darkness and the veil of pain.

love that is the luminous beauty of the human Soul. To awaken the Soul center is to reclaim this treasure.

One cannot speak of this time in a child's life as being a very long one, for the distractions of today's world are thrust very early onto our children. It used to be that an infant was kept quiet and protected. Now, there is only noise and stimulation. Is it any wonder that when the pain veil begins to grow, Soul embraces it as a wall, a buffer against the toxicity surrounding her? This is particularly true if there is a great deal of anger in the family, either expressed or repressed, for Soul feels the energy around her. Far from being welcomed into the world, she finds the world assaulting her, making it difficult for her to simply *be*. If she is unable to *be*, how can she ever relax and fully anchor in the human body?

Sometimes these early distractions are so terrible that from the moment many Souls enter this world, they focus on only one thing—how to leave it. Young people who contemplate or commit suicide are the result of Soul disappearing into the arms of pain. The pain veil seduces Soul with thoughts of non-being—of death—and to the illogical Soul this seems perfectly logical. To her there is no fear of death, for she is immortal and knows it. Only the presence of Spirit, and his veil of fear, keeps her here.

The infant, like Soul herself, is helpless and needs to be taken care of. This remains true of the Soul even into adulthood. Furthermore, she *wants* to be taken care of. This is her embarrassing secret, for even as she remains the part of you that secretly wants to be taken care of, she has been taught by life that it is wrong to be helpless—that she should be powerful and strong. Power and strength—these are attributes of God, not Soul. So while she may try very hard to exhibit these masculine qualities, she is destined to continually fail. She fails not because she is not good enough or smart enough, but because the essential truth for Soul is that she is *meant* to be taken care of by Spirit and God, both of whom are close by her.

Unfortunately, as we grow away from childhood, our Spirit and God become captured by ego darkness, enmeshed in their own veils of fear and anger. Soul's perfect mate, the Spirit within, looks at her through a veil of fear. He fears love, the beautiful Soul of love. Is it any wonder that Soul seems overwhelmed and confused, when inside the beautiful Spirit, the perfect mate she searches for outside, fears her—sees her through the veil of fear, forever keeping her separate. The obvious truths of helplessness, vulnerability and the need to be protected become hidden and even condemned later in life, but they are truths nonetheless. They dissolve as issues only with the awakening of God, and His realization that all along, he was supposed to protect and take care of Soul.

Until the God center awakens—as long as He is controlled by ego anger—He will be the part inside each of us that is condemning, judging Soul for being weak and helpless, calling her a hopeless romantic and dreamer divorced from reality. Only with the awakening of God is Soul's place in the world finally secure.

Soul is also the inner scapegoat, the part of us that receives all blame and condemnation from within and without. This ancient role of the Soul is indicated in creation scripture. It was Eve who yielded to the temptation of the Serpent. It was Eve, the feminine Soul, who was blamed for the fall from paradise, and she has been blamed ever since. Strangely, there is a logical reason for Eve's fateful choice. The human Soul is the love center, and love has no "*no*". It is in a state of unconditional "*yes*" to existence. You will notice this state as the part of you that cannot say "no". You have tried to fix this flaw, or condemned it. "Why did I say yes?" you ask yourself.

If you were in your Soul center and you were asked for a favor, or a salesman befriended you before delivering his sales pitch, you *will* say yes. You will do this not because you are weak or stupid, but because you are in your Soul center. You are in your "*yes*". Scripture does not indicate that Eve is evil. The deeper truth is that she cannot say "no". So the story of Eve and the Serpent does not point to the evil of the feminine, but points instead to the innocence, goodness, and perfection of Soul's love.

Soul is also the shy one inside of us, the most hidden part of who we are. We reveal her, if at all, only to special people and in special moments. It is she who connects to the mystery that is intended to anchor

Soul is also the shy one inside of us, the most hidden part of who we are. We reveal her, if at all, only to special people and in special moments.

us to life. People whom we sometimes think of as being 'spacey', or who experience themselves drifting out of their bodies, or even having out-of-body episodes, are manifesting conditions of Soul that relate to her inability to be in the world. It is understandable that if the pain and its subsequent feeling of separation makes life unbearable to the human Soul, it would appear perfectly logical to her to leave it. If she happens to discover drugs, or if meditation techniques seem to open a door to enable her to drift in dream worlds, or if she can actually leave the body entirely, these are very powerful and memorable experiences. Though she might be helpless in the material world, in subtler worlds she is very powerful indeed.

Once discovering a key to release, even temporary release, from the ego prison, she will not forget it. She will attempt to open the door again and again in order to escape, but will only find herself sinking deeper and deeper into addiction. When you condemn yourself for weakness, laziness, clumsiness, stupidity and addiction, you are in all likelihood condemning your Soul. If you are an addict, then condemning her will more likely drive her deeper into addiction.

To put it succinctly, God is attacking and blaming the very Soul he promised to protect for all the failure in life. It is as though a tree were to expend all its energy attacking, condemning, hacking away at its roots, blaming them for the tree's inability to grow strong, flower, and take its rightful place in creation. If such a tree existed, it would seem mad to you. And yet that is what is happening to everyone possessed by ego madness. One part, strong and powerful, God, is deceived into attacking and blaming the most sensitive, innocent part for all failures in life. This is how the ego mindlessly turns us against ourselves. It is an inner war of destruction that is projected outside as well. Hell inside. Hell outside.

The Soul center is also that place of exquisite tenderness, where we can touch and merge with other souls, such as when we make love. It is the place where we feel grace, as though blessed from beyond. The exquisiteness of Soul becomes matter of fact in an awakened being. Different psychic gifts such as telepathy may appear as she awakens, though surprisingly, she is just as likely to disdain these gifts, as she is to embrace them. In all likelihood, she will be awakening into a world controlled by ego, a world that will continue to project conflicting thoughts to her. In an awakened state, she will receive messages very clearly. Awake, she is a delicate receiver, desirous of peace and quiet. But for a telepathic Soul, to receive the thoughts and feelings of others is like being in room full of radios and televisions, all loudly blaring trauma and drama. This when, after her long journey, all she desires is silence and peace. As the awakening deepens, Soul learns to utilize whatever gifts she holds in ways that serve, rather than disturb.

The Soul is the place of abandonment – that is, the place where abandonment is experienced.

The Soul is the place of abandonment—that is, the place where abandonment is experienced. Spirit shares this feeling with Soul, for Spirit fears abandonment. Literally, Spirit fears Soul disappearing into the pain veil, getting lost in the pain of abandonment. Scripture seems to indicate that abandonment began in the garden, when Soul and Spirit were cast out of paradise, abandoned by God. This is an incorrect interpretation. God has never abandoned Soul and Spirit. He is there, inside, where he has always been, hidden behind a veil of anger.

But for Soul, the ejection from the garden is *experienced* as abandonment, and living as she does in a timeless, boundless world, it is as though the events of the Fall happened yesterday. In fact, she has felt abandoned with such regularity, that she long ago began to expect being abandoned. Her reality in ego darkness is that whenever she connects with anyone, they will eventually leave her—they will abandon her. To Soul, this seems preordained.

It *is* preordained, for the ego pain will insure that it is so. As Soul's light moves through the pain veil to connect with another person, the pain always reminds her that the 'other' will leave—will abandon her. Even as Soul's energy seeks to connect, it is already corrupted, encoded with an expectation that the one with whom she seeks to connect will leave her. Though she wants these connections to last forever, it becomes her expectation that they will not. If she expects to be abandoned, she will be. Existence simply responds to her expectations. It cannot be otherwise. Where will Soul wind up after she is abandoned? She will be in the comforting arms of her pain—the very thing responsible for her abandonment. The pain will whisper *I told you so*, as it once again feeds off her perfect love and transforms it into darkness—a lonely Hell.

The reason that Soul's sense of abandonment goes so deep is that it is a constantly re-occurring echo of what she has misinterpreted as the first abandonment by God. As I have pointed out, God did not abandon her. Rather, as the veil of pain descended around her (just as the veil of fear descended around Spirit), a long gradual separation occurred. In other words, abandonment is a misinterpretation of the gradual separation that occurred as the three centers of consciousness disappeared further and further into their veils of ego separation.

The Soul center is also that place of mysterious longing that even the presence of a lover cannot quell. This deep longing is sometimes focused on a lover, on family or community, but it is so deep and ongoing that no matter how connected you feel in life, this longing never really goes away. At best, it is the longing for home—

The Soul center is also that place of mysterious longing that even the presence of a lover cannot quell.

that is, the feeling of home. This longing will not disappear until Soul and Spirit are awakened and back in Eden Consciousness. The awakened Soul recognizes home, and begins to understand that she was never abandoned, she never sinned, and she was never bad or evil.

The Soul is the part of us most associated with the body, since Soul anchors us to existence by anchoring in the body. This vessel has been called the temple of the Soul, implying holiness by virtue of what it contained. One way to gauge your attitude towards Soul, to understand how the ego illusion has distorted your relationship with her, simply examine your attitudes to your own body. For most people, Soul's experience of body is a nightmare. Everywhere, manipulators from the beauty, fashion and healthcare industries, encourage rejection of the body. Far from being thought of as the temple it once was, it has now become the enemy. In this distorted world our bodies are not pretty enough, strong enough, healthy enough— in short, they are not perfect. Even the so-called 'beautiful people' reject the physical body. Models starve themselves, torturing and punishing and destroying, trying to attain some unattainable ego idea of perfection. Once you have been awakened, you discover that your body was always the perfect temple for you.

There are many ego masks through which soul looks and interacts with the material world—beliefs, conditions, rules supplied by family, church, society, and the media. All offer ready- made identities for Soul to assume. She has no choice. They are forced upon her, and in her innocence she accepts and assumes them. I will speak briefly about a few of these Soul identities, in order to help you identify your Soul states, to understand when you are in your Soul center, and to help you become familiar with them.

One of most common identities, or masks, is that of the romantic. If you consider yourself a romantic, then when you are in romantic thoughts or dreams filled with hope, or in gloomy thoughts and dreams filled with loneliness and despair, you are in your Soul center. You are looking out through layers of sadness, either at the ego dream of hope, of love fulfilled, or at the ego dream of despair, of love denied.

It is natural for Soul to seek love, for without it, she is not alive. She longs to feel that sense of aliveness that only comes with love, when her light and energy flow through the body and into the world. Though this feeling is exhilarating, it nevertheless contains the seeds of its own corruption. For the romantic is nothing but ego patterning and a set of beliefs about love.

Every romantic has certain romantic conditions, and since every ego is patterned differently, each ego romantic has different conditions about what constitutes love. To insure that the lover will fail these conditions, most of them are hidden. Nevertheless, holidays provide some obvious examples. Valentine's day is a day like any other—you may feel in a loving mood that day, you may not. But woe unto you if you neglect to shower the loved one with special attention and gifts on that day. Only the most adept romantic will navigate this one safely.

Each romantic is assured of failure in love by the nature of ego conditions. These conditions have nothing to do with love, and everything to do with pain. If you are not attentive on Valentine's Day you will be accused of hurting the beloved.

Every romantic has certain romantic conditions, and since every ego is patterned differently, each ego romantic has different conditions about what constitutes love. To insure that the lover will fail these conditions, most of them are hidden.

Ego's beliefs about love are learned *beliefs* about how to do something imperfectly, clumsily, that your Soul already knows how to do perfectly, impeccably. Learned beliefs about love are different in each culture, and in fact differ from individual to individual. The single thing that can be said about the ego beliefs and conditions surrounding love is that they make love impossibly difficult and confusing. Fortunately, we have no end of experts to instruct us. Unfortunately, Soul is not a worker. The more difficult you make love, the less your Soul will be there. She has a naïve belief that love should be simple, and of course Soul is right. It is simple and easy to love the pain surrounding her—it is difficult and impossible to love anyone through the pain—through the ego conditions and walls defending the pain.

No one can figure out hidden conditions of the ego romantic, and when they are or are not met. If they are not met, ego will punish you by withholding love and denying you Soul's light. Over time, love will disappear because it was not love being nourished or protected, but rather the veil of pain. The ego romantic is a minefield, impossible to navigate. The Soul, perfectly loving and sustaining the ego, will be rewarded with failure, heartache, and blame.

There is one simple fundamental to understand about Soul and relationships—this is, that she has a secret, ancient lover, who has never abandoned her. This lover is pain. Pain doesn't want Soul to love anyone else, for without her love, pain would die. And so whenever Soul attempts to love anyone outside, this secret lover inside whispers *"they will hurt you"—"they don't really love you"—"you aren't good enough"—"you aren't pretty enough"*. Endless messages sent from an ancient evil voice to the innocent Soul.

The ego dreams of love are based, as is ego itself, in pain. One could describe love dreams as anti-pain dreams, dreams that hold the promise of love, hope, and an end to pain and loneliness. We say that hope is eternal, but it is only as eternal as the pain from which it springs. Those who have loved, have experienced the remembrance of love's ending as an awakening from a dream, as though hope and love were the illusion, and pain and loneliness the reality. In fact, pain is the heart of the illusion from which the hope, and the dreams of love are generated. This is why, as the dreamy Soul awakens, what she first experiences is loss of hope. Then she experiences loss of pain. Hope is the ego projection into the future—the thing that helps us avoid what appears to be the present—pain. So, in awakening to the present moment, first we experience losing the future projection, which is hope. Then we experience its place of origin, the pain. In the end Soul is left in the present moment, which is the only reality there is.

In this simple state of *beingness*, if love appears, she is ready. If love disappears, that is also acceptable, for awake, the Soul is what she has always been—unconditional love. She is no longer starved by the pain veil, no longer needy for love, no longer a beggar. She is more like a flower, releasing her fragrance whether or not there is anyone to appreciate or receive it.

Another ego mask is the caregiver. This is a natural expression of Soul, for in man she is the natural conduit of the mother, the goddess ... existence. Through Soul, existence strives to take care of other souls. We are all connected, or we used to be long ago. Without ego, existence would take care of all of us, seeing that the perfect person would be there at the perfect moment, with perfect assistance. Soul can understand this, for unless she is totally lost in the ego darkness, she still believes in magic. She might even have dim memories of lives filled with magic.

Ego has destroyed the magic that used to exist, and replaced with the *soul-lessness* of science and technology. As Soul has been driven from the world, so has magic—the easy interaction with the natural world. As she has been driven from the world, so have mystery, holiness, and the sacredness of existence.

The caregiver, being a natural expression of Soul in the world, used to be drawn naturally to healthcare, a field that has now been taken over by science and technology. Science has created miracles, but healthcare is now a business—rushed, disconnected, artificial and uncaring. As the natural intuitive healer within, Soul seeks harmony and balance. She knows intuitively that harmony and balance are the sources of health and well-being. When you are feeling ill, your natural inclination is to withdraw—to minimize noise and stimulation, and seek quiet and rest. But in the ego world, time is money, and money is the god we worship. Instead of following Soul's wisdom, we act more like machines rather than delicate natural beings. Soul's gentle healing skills are no longer valued. Rather than become technocrats and slaves to machines, caregiver Souls instead leave the healthcare professions, where like so many professions formerly open to

The caregiver, being a natural expression of Soul in the world, used to be drawn naturally to healthcare, a field that has now been taken over by science and technology.

Soul, she is no longer valued—she is not efficient, you see.

Reflect on your life—on how much time the healer within has spent lost in depression, listening to ego darkness. Those times when Soul energy has been consumed by the pain veil, generating negative thoughts about your life and your body. Has Soul ever felt at home, relaxed and accepting in your body? Reflect too on how much of your own inner healer's energy has been transformed into rejection of your body, and you will see just a glimmer of the damage that ego is doing to your health. Recent discoveries of the effects of stress on the body are just the tip of the iceberg. Ego is the spiritual *dis*-ease that is creating the majority of physical diseases.

For those who cannot afford America's healthcare system, there is an alternative. That alternative is *awakening*. If you remove the veils that are destroying your energy, you will experience your body coming into harmony for the first time. As long as the veils are in place, they will constantly stress your body with negativity. The ego transforms the beautiful light of God into a mindless, dis-harmonious chaos, never ever allowing the physical body to operate harmoniously. Without harmony and balance the body is always in a state of *dis*-ease. If one's ego patterning is such that there is a total rejection of the body, then the power of the God within is being used to attack it. Awakened, you will look back and wonder that your body was able to survive the constant assaults and poisonings of the ego experience.

Some caregivers give compulsively. In the world of ego patterns, such a caregiver is someone who never receives—they do not know how to receive. In the ego world of impossible conditions, such a Soul is not allowed to receive until everyone else is taken care of. A Soul so obsessed will never attain this goal, because it is unattainable. As a result, she will never receive.

Another mask of the Soul is the <u>victim</u>. When this mask appears, you are very close to the pain veil—very close to Soul herself. This is the darkest mask, for it is closest to the darkness shrouding the human Soul. The victim is a black hole of neediness, helplessness, and vulnerability. One's Soul is instinctively drawn to a victim, because she sees not only another Soul, but also her own inner lover—her own pain.

In fact, when we say in empathy 'I feel your pain', it is not an accurate statement. What we are really feeling is our own pain, pulsating in resonance to another Soul's pain. You cannot feel another's pain until your own wall of pain is removed. Though it is then possible, once a Soul has been liberated, she

In fact, when we say in empathy 'I feel your pain', it is not an accurate statement. What we are really feeling is our own pain, pulsating in resonance to another Soul's pain.

does not want to connect with another's pain. Once she understands the reality of the pain, it would be illogical for her to want to connect to and feed the ego tormenting another Soul, no matter how much that other Soul lost in darkness might want or demand it. To give attention to another Soul's pain—to feed its pain—is to simply strengthen the pain veil tormenting that Soul. In such a case, the ego illusion feeds not only off of the Soul inside, but also on the Soul feeding it from outside.

None of the love or energy that you give reaches the hurting Soul unless the Soul herself actually appears, in which case there will be felt a deep love and tenderness. That is why some people seem to be energy vampires, needing attention that seems to disappear into a bottomless hole. You cannot heal their pain veil. It consumes love to exist, and the more you love it, the greater its appetite. Victims will cause burnout in caregivers more quickly than anything else, for Soul is delicate and can be quickly depleted if not protected.

Soul has been taught that pain is there to teach her lessons about love, caring, tenderness and sensitivity, and over time, pain assumed a spiritual patina, an aura of holiness. Suffering and self-sacrifice were taught as virtues, paths to holiness and perfection. If anything in this life could be called holy, it would be the human Soul, but as the ego darkness deepened and Soul's light disappeared into the dark veil of pain, the pain itself began to claim the mantle of holiness, while Soul seemingly disappeared from existence.

Pain has nothing to teach your Soul. Pain begets pain, isolation, loneliness and despair. It is not holy. It is, instead, the very heart of the evil within.

8. The God Center

The God center is located in the area of the third eye. The essence of this center is truth. The part of you that takes truth very seriously, that part is your God, trying to hold dear His essence—truth.

Into each life is born a Spirit of trust, a Soul of love, and a God of truth. Perhaps you can remember your childhood lessons about truth. Like most children, you were taught to tell the truth. It is the nature of the God in the child not yet corrupted, to tell the truth. But lessons imparted with the best intentions about the value of truth, are early on at odds with the lessons of experience.

For instance, the child-God learns that many times when he speaks the truth, it causes embarrassment and conflict for his parents. How many children are actually, sincerely praised for telling the truth? Overtly or covertly his parents' inner Gods cannot avoid becoming angry and blaming the child. Even if this anger is not overtly expressed, the child knows, and may feel guilty and fearful. That is, his Soul begins to slip into the veil of pain, and his Spirit begins to slip into the veil of fear. The child may also experience confusion and frustration as he tries to make sense of the conflicting messages he is receiving. Thus, as the anger veil begins to appear, the child God instinctively embraces it.

In growing anger, the child-God seeks to reconcile his actual knowledge of truth with the confusing, contradictory, ego distortions of truth. He is not stupid—even in a child's body. This is an ancient God, an intelligent God, and it doesn't take the child-God long to discern the fundamentals of truth in an ego-driven world, the most fundamental being: *truth equals punishment*. That is, whenever parents,

> *It doesn't take the child-God long to discern the fundamentals of truth in an ego-driven world, the most fundamental being: truth equals punishment.*

teachers, or other adults demand the truth, it is not because truth has some fundamental value in itself. Rather, these other Gods want the child-God to acknowledge *their* view of the truth. They do not want to instruct in the value of the sanctity of truth, but rather they seek an excuse to blame and punish for disagreement. The child-God learns early on that whenever truth is demanded of him, it is often the prelude to, and the justification for, punishment. Thus, the lesson learned is a simple one—truth leads to blame and punishment.

While the child is being indoctrinated in the confusing ego values surrounding truth, he witnesses the adults around him lying, deceiving, and distorting truth to serve their own purposes. They do this even as they are attempting to impart the moral and ethical values that they hold dear, to the child.

God learns his lessons well. By the time of adolescence, when the child-God begins to emerge as a major player in life, he has become expert in deception, lies, and blame. In preparation for his entry into the larger world, the child-

God has mastered the blame game and become completely disconnected from his essence, which is truth. He enters the world hardened, cynical, angry, alienated, and ready to point the finger of blame at everyone—at parents, friends, lovers, bosses, coworkers, enemies—even at the world itself.

The lessons that the child-God learned about the corruption of truth, he will pass on to his own children. Thus the creative and blessing God disappears once again into ego corruption, as these false truths are unknowingly passed on to a new generation of child-Gods who are guided and mentored in the schizophrenic world where truth, far from setting you free, appears to have exactly the opposite effect.

This endless tradition of passing on an angry God to subsequent generations is not meant to be an indictment of parents. That would be a misinterpretation, for parents are already so crippled by their own ego illusions they cannot help but pass them on to their children. Unless a parent has a conscious intent to destroy a child, I am against blaming parents for the dysfunction of their offspring. However twisted and distorted that intent may become as it is expressed through ego distortion, every parent intends to do the best for their children.

Furthermore, although every child is born in innocence, he is also born with the seeds of corruption. These seeds are the veils, which are dormant at birth. As the light of consciousness begins to flow through them they respond to it and they grow. Even with enlightened parents, Soul's love light would dim as the pain veil began to grow, Spirit's trust light would dim as the fear veil began to grow, and God's truth light would once again disappear into anger.

What happened to God? How can the angry vengeful tyrant inside of you be God? He is not fair, or just, or compassionate. What happened to change Him? The answer is simple. He created some companions—the human Soul, Eve, and the human Spirit, Adam.

God took His love, compassion, and caring to create Soul. He took His trust, fairness and playfulness to create Spirit.

God created them out of Himself. He took His love, compassion, and caring to create Soul. He took His trust, fairness and playfulness to create Spirit. The God who entered the garden was one. The God who left the garden, the God inside each of us, is divided into three parts, each containing an essence, a single quality of the divine. The essence of Soul is love. The essence of Spirit is trust. The essence of God is truth.

With these three centers of consciousness held separate and in conflict by the ego veils, you can experience the world entirely through your God center, but you will be neither loving and compassionate (Soul) nor fair and trusting (Spirit). You will, instead, be arbitrary and arrogant. You can and do shift from center to center, as though angry, critical and blaming in one moment (God), and in the next moment tearful, guilty and vulnerable (Soul). Or perhaps you shift to your Spirit center, through which you will listen and seek conciliation rather than simply laying down the law (God).

You can easily distinguish these three parts in yourself or in others—all one has to do is look. The phony ego mask will be deceptive, but just ask yourself, 'what lies behind the mask?' Is it anger? Is it fear or pain? In metaphysical terms, there are three great thrones inside each of us. They are occupied by Soul, Spirit, and God. There is an illustration of the enthroned God on the dollar bill—the pyramid of the great seal with a capstone of an open eye—the symbol of the awakened God on his throne.

However, in today's world there is a usurper on God's throne, and this usurper is anger. It is not unlike an evil advisor who whispers to the king, trying through his deviousness to control the king and his kingdom. In most Gods today, anger doesn't just sit beside God on his throne, it actually occupies the throne, ruling in *Though God is not stupid, he is made so by the anger – an ancient advisor that over time has grown in power and influence, making God weak and powerless.* the name and with the power of God. Unfortunately, in the age of science and technology, we have no wizards who can instantly overthrow the usurper, as they can in fairytales. God must actually work, develop some awareness, in order to banish the usurper and regain His rightful place in both the material world and the inner world.

Though God is not stupid, he is made so by the anger— an ancient advisor that over time has grown in power and influence, making God weak and powerless. One reason God is so attached to his anger is that he feels powerless without it. But like all the veils, there is a deception—without God the anger has no power. That is, the power God feels in the anger is

His own power, not the power of the anger. Simply remember how even when your own God feels most powerful when He is in the anger, he simultaneously feels powerless. God, who is powerful, gives his power to the anger. This makes God feel powerless and impotent, even as God's own anger gives Him the *illusion* of power.

The anger also sends a deceptive message to God. *Of course you're angry,* it says. *Anyone facing a similar situation would be angry.* In other words, anger justifies its existence to the very thing that is unwittingly controlled by it—your inner God.

If the God inside of you wants to know why He feels so powerless, He just needs to be alert. The next time He storms about something, ask yourself if whatever seemingly annoyed God is really worthy of His attention, or if it is instead something so petty as to be beneath Him. Perhaps your God gets angry about loftier issues, like politics, religion, corporate greed or government corruption. These are legitimate concerns of God, but if He is alert, He will see there is very little He can actually do except, perhaps, to stew hour after hour in that ugliness that is the anger. The point I wish to make is that every moment God is lost in anger, steaming over petty issues, his power, intelligence, and creativity are pouring into that corruption, making him feel ugly, mean, vindictive and powerless. Of course he feels powerless. The anger has consumed his power and transported him from perfection, into an ugly, violent nightmare.

More anger, less God. More anger, less creativity. More

anger, less intelligence. God, who keeps the books inside, detailing credits and debits in the world of good and evil, is so blinded by the anger veil that the simple math of this equation escapes him. His relationship with the anger is a deal with the devil, and God, who prides Himself on His business acumen, has been taken for a ride on a cosmic scale.

God needs to reflect on those situations in life that He regrets to this day. He needs to ask whether or not whatever was said or done in the past was said or done in anger. God doesn't like to think he is stupid, because he is not. But the ego veils, being the opposite of what they surround, are stupid in equal measure to the intelligence that is poured into them to give them light and sustenance. As an advisor to God, the anger veil is easily revealed for what it actually is—petty, mean, condemning, judgmental, cruel and unbelievably stupid.

God is the place of generosity. All Gods think of themselves as being generous, and many are. It is part of God's nature to be generous. But generosity too moves through ego corruption, with the result that no gift is given freely

Only an awakened God can give a gift unconditionally, without expectation of a gift in return.

or unconditionally. The ego is always keeping books and lists, chronicles of its own experience of the world of good and evil—lists of scores to settle, revenge to be meted out, and the monetary list—what has been given, what has not been received in return. Only an awakened God can give a gift unconditionally, without expectation of a gift in return. A gift is a gift, not an investment or a transaction. In the ego world, true gifts have disappeared. The great God of creation, reduced to being a petty corrupt accountant, devotes his attention and energy to pouring over lists of ancient slights, insults, and inequalities.

This is the gift the ego anger has bestowed on the great God who created, and is in everything visible, in this, his creation. The anger, the ancient evil and trusted advisor, has turned God into the enslaver and destroyer of His own creation. If you think slavery has disappeared,

All religions are created by God, and wherever there is an ideological belief system that seeks to control and manipulate people, it is His creation.

consider this—would you go to work today if not for the economic slavery imposed by the true religion that dominates Western thought—Capitalism? In the ego world of good and evil, Capitalism shares with all religions the properties to deliver both good and evil. All religions are created by God, and wherever there is an ideological belief system that seeks to control and manipulate people, it is His creation.

These many religions are always at war with each other. We no sooner end the holy war between Capitalism and Communism, than another holy war appears—this time of more traditional nature, between recognized traditional religions. As John F. Kennedy said, "All wars are holy wars". But why? They are all holy wars simply by virtue of who is fighting them—God. Angry self-righteous Gods fighting angry self-righteous Gods, husbands fighting wives, Democrats fighting Republicans, fundamentalists fighting secular humanists, New Age believers fighting traditionalists, workers fighting management, women fighting men, homosexuals fighting heterosexuals—all angry, fighting Gods. What un-winnable holy wars are distracting your own angry God as His creation is being destroyed?

Each warring God believes He is on the side of good, and that the opposing God is on the side of evil. None of these Gods is awakened. Sleeping Gods are fighting on both sides, each convinced by the anger veil of their own rightness and virtue. They mindlessly go on destroying the real world and its real inhabitants, in service to false, illusionary ideologies and beliefs given to them by others. They are brainwashed, just as innocent children are brainwashed with the promise of 75 virgins and passage to Paradise, into becoming suicide bombers. All to impose a particular ideological slavery upon humanity.

As long as the anger veil controls your God, He will be endlessly engaged in holy wars, both petty and monumental. I suggest a holy war more worthy of His attention, a war that He can really win—the war to destroy *As long as the anger veil controls your God, He will be endlessly engaged in holy wars, both petty and monumental.* the ego illusion within. In this war God is assured of victory. He is, after all, God, and ego is His creation, and therefore can never be *more* powerful than Him. Might this not be the perfect time to reclaim Eden and liberate his children, Soul and Spirit, from ancient darkness, and regain the love and respect he lost so long ago?

The anger veil claims to show God the truth, and in most

cases it does. Not that the anger has insight into truth—the
anger is an illusion—it can no more know truth than it can
know love or trust. It cannot *know* anything. Look not to the
anger to reveal truth, but rather to the God looking *through*
the veil of anger, the God whose essence *is* truth. Wherever an
awakened God looks, He sees Himself—He sees truth. That
which determines truth is God *looking*, not the anger veil which
is simply *directing* God where to look. If my anger directs my
God to look and listen to the Israelis, I will see truth there. But
if it directs me to look there, it does not allow me to see or hear
the truth spoken by the Palestinians, also sleeping Gods, also
speaking truth.

In entering the anger veil, God entered a world artificially
divided into good and evil. Anger directs God where to look
and what to hear, and does not allow Him to look elsewhere
or hear anything different. This is why an angry person will
not hear a word you are saying, nor will he see where you
are pointing. The ego *is* the divided world of good and evil.
It is impossible for ego to concede that two opposing sides or
viewpoints could *both* be true.

Only in an awakened state is God able to look everywhere
and hear everything. What God finds is Himself—truth
everywhere. He is no longer forced by the anger to take sides
in the endless holy wars over truth. He becomes once again
free. Once free, he discovers what has eluded him for so
long—peace.

In the ego world, stripped of power by the anger veil, God
perceives that the only way to reclaim the power He has lost

is with money. Even the most pious televangelist focuses on money. It is the universal God of our age. God sees other Gods with great power, in direct proportion to the amount of wealth they have amassed. In the world of ego deception, God is deceived into believing that wealth will restore His power, bring back the respect He has lost, and of course furnish a universal currency with which to buy love. It is unfortunate that only the rich are able to know the emptiness of this deception.

If God is successful in gaining wealth, it will buy power and domination over others, but His kingdom will be peopled with slaves. They will respect Him to His face, but envy and despise Him behind his back. They will pretend to love Him. Being intelligent, God will know their respect is false and will disappear without money, as will their false love. Having exhausted the possibilities of redemption in ego world, God will eventually slip into defeat and bitterness. I am not against money—nor am I saying that you must eschew money. Once awakened, you will still be in a world dominated by ego. But in your new wisdom you will be able to use money, not be used by it.

God is the part that looks down on people. A smart God knows He should not do this, and tries to hide His arrogance. But this trait is true of all fallen Gods, and like all aspects kept in denial, it is important to recognize. It is an ego distortion of truth. There is a natural basis for the tendency of God to look down on the mortals around Him. His center is in the forehead, the third eye, and His physical relationship with the two human centers of consciousness, is that they exist below Him on the human body. Soul resides in the heart, and Spirit resides in the solar plexus.

God watches over them from above, and from there He looks down at them. This is why Soul and Spirit always feel as if they are being judged from above, because in the world of the body, judgment does come from above them. In the natural world there is no judgment. In other words, an awakened God does not look down with contempt. He simply looks. From His throne He looks to the thrones of Soul and Spirit. In the divided, conflicted world of ego, this becomes distorted, and God finds Himself looking down with contempt on humanity.

God is the part inside who is above rules, and above the law. Laws are written by angry Gods, supposedly to protect us. But laws have a curious side effect. In the ego world of good and evil, every law that is written with the intent to protect us, also diminishes our freedom. Every law that is written to ensure our safety and well-being, simultaneously diminishes our freedom and enslaves us. There are so many laws in America, one cannot exist without breaking them daily, often without even trying.

Every God believes that laws are meant for all the other Gods, and that they do not really apply to Him. He is God, who makes the laws within for Soul and Spirit. Laws may apply to a husband, wife or child, but not to the God within. He is above the law. Nevertheless, when not totally possessed by the anger veil, God is intelligent, and understands the necessity of rules to govern life. But when you are running a stop sign or cheating on your taxes, it is your God doing it. It is not Soul.

It is not Spirit, whose very fear is used by the law to control him. Generally, it is God who breaks the law. For ordinary folk, this usually means small harmless incursions into the world of lawlessness. But for wealthy powerful Gods, lawlessness can reach catastrophic proportions, particularly when those Gods are in charge of corporations or governments.

In relationships, God is absent in the beginning. After all, in the beginning one tries to put one's best face forward. An angry God with His ugly face wisely remains hidden in the background. Though hidden, He busies Himself keeping the books—that is, recording the list of transgressions of the hidden relationship rules. The partner, not privy to this demonic rulebook, naturally will make mistakes. God also records the hot buttons for pain and fear for future use, for he always seeks to strike at the most vulnerable places—Soul and Spirit.

When the honeymoon period ends, God begins to appear. Once angry Gods appear in a relationship, it is usually the beginning of the end. When arguments erupt, partners are stunned to have their words and actions from long ago thrown in their faces, leaving them asking *where did this come from?* An angry God has a long memory, crammed with the slights of a lifetime, and He is always ready for revenge. His revenge will most likely be aimed at Soul (to hurt), or Spirit (to scare), threatening the security of the relationship. If both Gods in the relationship are successful in meting out punishment to Soul and Spirit, love and trust will be destroyed. Remaining will be two bickering Gods, connecting only in endless blame, neither hearing the other, both blind to the insanity they are causing, having the same argument over and over again. Nothing is heard, nothing resolved. Eventually, one or both Gods will simply end it.

The most common trait of all ego relationships is that love is not nourished—it is crushed. Usually, the poor innocent Soul is left with blame and guilt. Somehow in the ego world, inexplicably, it will all be her fault. With another relationship gone, she will find comfort in the arms of pain. The tragedy of it all is that God, the great destroyer of love and life, never chose to destroy anything. That decision was made by the anger. God has become the lackey of mindless, ego anger.

> *The most common trait of all ego relationships is that love is not nourished – it is crushed.*

9. Passing Through the Veils

As you contemplate the journey home, the first obstacle that you will encounter is the ego fear of change. How will your life change? What are you likely to lose? Obviously, life *will* change after you have awakened. But life will also change if you do not awaken, for change is the only constant in life. The great difference will be in the quality and direction of that change. In the ego world, change tends to be circular. The settings and costumes change in the story of your life, but the play remains the same, since the ego patterns directing it remain the same. Outwardly things may look different, but inwardly everything feels the same. After beginning to awaken, everything is different. You will no longer be moving in a circle, but spiraling inward, dissolving patterns as you move towards your true centers—Soul, Spirit and God. Outwardly all can remain the same, but the inward experience of life begins to change dramatically.

There are no prerequisites to begin your journey. There is nothing to deny or renounce, and nothing new to embrace. All that you *need* to know is within you, and meditation alone is enough to lead you to it. You do not even need to believe in God, Soul or Spirit. I use God, Soul and Spirit because they are the original identities given to one consciousness that has been divided and separated into three. As such, they are the deepest, most powerful identities in us, and to become aware of them is to light a beacon deep within that will guide you home. They are the gates to *oneness*—the gates to Paradise—the gates to home. Yet even God, Soul and Spirit are part of life's illusion, and if you are successful in awakening, they will be revealed as such.

The only change that is necessary to begin and safely navigate the journey home is a fundamental change in your relationship with the veils. You must be absolutely clear that

The only change that is necessary to begin and safely navigate the journey home is a fundamental change in your relationship with the veils.

fear, pain and anger are not your friends or trusted advisors. They are the opposite—the very enemies of life itself. The change that transforms everything is to accept pain and fear as the realities they are—that is, as uncomfortable physical sensations in your body. Instead of getting lost in them, spinning in circles and searching for some elusive meaning or lesson that they are supposed to be teaching, you must learn to recognize and observe them. You must begin to watch these sensations whenever they are present. This change in your relationship to the pain and fear veils will ignite the process of awakening and open all doors to the treasure within.

The concept of *watching* is very difficult to convey, though once you 'get it' it is obvious. Suppose you have a paper cut on your hand. The sensation it produces immediately draws your awareness to it, as it should. The sensation makes you aware that something is wrong and requires action. Perhaps you put a bandage on the cut and resume your activities. You are aware from time to time of the injury when your awareness is drawn back by the sensation. Are you the sensation, or are you the one aware of it? In other words, do you become totally identified with the cut, as though the totality of *you* is the cut? Or are you somewhat detached—aware of and observing the sensation present in your physical body? The veils are merely uncomfortable sensations present in your physical body. The only difference between the veils and the paper cut is that you become them totally, and get lost in the ego mythology about them generated in your mind by the sensations. You are aware of your thoughts *about* the sensations, rather than the sensations themselves.

To watch these veils is to become aware of the actual sensation we label *pain*, the actual sensation we label *fear*. To watch them is to observe them with detachment, neither for nor against—to observe them with the detachment of a scientist, as very curious, uncomfortable physical sensations. This is what I mean by *watching*.

If you want to succeed, the process of awakening must be placed first on your list of life priorities. With the information contained in this book, any individual with sufficient motivation can awaken. Those things that are not in this narrative will be revealed to you on the journey, as you need them. Because every ego is different, each individual path home is also different, and it is impossible to anticipate all contingencies. Some individual Gods, those who are very controlling about everything, including their spiritual journey, will insist on doing it their way, with no outside assistance. To me, this is very hard and punishing. But it is not up to me to question the wisdom of a fallen God. Ultimately, however you do it, it will

If you want to succeed, the process of awakening must be placed first on your list of life priorities.

mysteriously be revealed as the perfect way—the only way for you, no matter how hard it may appear to others. The most important thing is to follow your intuition (Soul) in all matters concerning your journey.

Despite having said this, I do not recommend undertaking the journey alone. The best and most auspicious approach is to work with a guide, one who has already awakened—one who has navigated the ego labyrinth and knows the way home. Such a guide knows that the ego is cunning and will want to distract you and derail the process. Such a guide will be aware of the hidden ego desire to become enlightened, may even feed it in the beginning to help you get going on the journey, only to starve it at the end. For the ego cannot be enlightened. But there are places on the journey where the ego will believe it has attained enlightenment, and the closer you get to your goal, the greater the danger.

As you awaken you become more powerful, as whatever remains of the ego dies. But the ego, even while it is dissolving, continues to reform and re-create identities. The time of greatest danger is when you are in the spiritual ego identity—when you are clear and awake enough to mask and control the remaining ego corruption. In this spiritual identity you may believe yourself enlightened. You may have a practiced serenity and balance, perhaps a façade of holiness. You believe you are spiritual and enlightened, but you don't yet *know*. Doubt lingers like a shadow, and will serve you well. For this spiritual identity, like other ego identities, sets you apart and above other mortals. Thus you are still in the duality of good and evil. The ego will want you to stop at this point, as though saying to you, *this state is better than anything you have known—why risk disturbing it—why go further?*

You must successfully transcend this spiritual identity and slip into what I refer to as *is*-ness. True enlightenment is very natural and ordinary—you might say that it is 'extraordinarily ordinary'. *Is*-ness refers to this quality of ordinariness. If you feel special and above others, then you are not yet home. An awakened guide will keep an eye on your progress, point out ego distractions, affirm the rightness of your path, and pull you back if you begin to slide into the spiritual ego identity.

> *True enlightenment is very natural and ordinary – you might say that it is 'extraordinarily ordinary'.*

Unfortunately, awakened guides are uncommon, and sometimes difficult to recognize among the myriad ego beliefs and confusion surrounding the concept of spirituality. However, your Soul, depending on her clarity and your trust of her, should know the right guide when he appears. If you seriously want to undertake this journey, and an awakened guide is not available, I recommend finding a few like-minded individuals and forming an 'awakening group'. In the absence of an individual awakened guide, from the beginning of the journey to the first breakthrough, which is Eden Consciousness, such a group is the safest, fastest, and most effective alternative. This should be a small working group, preferably with an odd number of participants, rather than a large discussion-type group.

Such groups should meet regularly—at least once a week—utilizing whatever tools and therapeutic techniques, however unorthodox, that members feel comfortable with. Serious work should be balanced with meditative tools such as the Tarot, which are not only fun, but which also encourage the development of intuitive skills. A distinct advantage of group work is that when one or more participants wanders off the path, lost in ego darkness, the others are still on the path, and can offer reassurance, clarity and support. The smaller the group, the more intense will be the processing of the ego veils and the attendant ego patterns, beliefs, and defenses.

As you move through the ego layers, you will be moving through and dissolving your own inner madness. Because this process can become very difficult, it is beneficial to have regular contact with others on the path. Companions who are on the same journey will give you the support and encouragement that will be sorely lacking in the ego dominated world. This companionship is most crucial from the beginning of your journey until you reach Eden Consciousness, the point at which your Soul and Spirit are both awake. Until you achieve this breakthrough, you will be journeying without benefit of clear centers of consciousness. You will be moving through darkness with only your intuition as an inner compass. Once you attain Eden Consciousness, you begin to enter the world of God. In awakening God, you begin to move alone, even if you are participating in a group. Every individual moves alone through the awakening of God—it is simply the nature of this part of the journey.

Soul is the most important center of consciousness for the journey. As I have already mentioned, intuition is the inner compass that points the way home, and intuition is seated in the human Soul. It is impossible to find the way back home without Soul, for how can one navigate through the ego illusion without a navigator—without someone who is able to intuit the rightness of choices, feel the correctness of the direction taken, and help when logical outward signs confuse or contradict the rightness of the path. The path to enlightenment is unique for every individual, and though each person may share with others the commonality of awakening the centers, each individual journey or experience as these centers awaken, is unique.

Intuition is the inner compass that points the way home, and intuition is seated in the human Soul.

Spirit and God are not intuitive. Both being masculine, they have a natural inclination to trust in what is objectively seen. Both have a natural tendency to trust logic and rationality, and experience and move through life in a linear way. While Soul's qualities are not valued in the material world, her seeing (intuition) becomes essential for navigating through the labyrinth of ego illusion to regain God's truth. While the path leads backwards from *omega* to *alpha*, it does not do so in a direct, lincar path.

Ego will present many distractions along the way. This is inevitable, and will ultimately be seen as 'perfect'. To the seeker, however, these distractions will cause confusion, doubt and conflict. *Am I proceeding correctly, or have I left the path?* Outwardly, as long as Spirit and God are watching the sensations when they appear, they are doing all they can do. Objective reality may appear better or worse, but for God especially, it will never look perfect (the way it should). Inwardly however, one accesses a subtler reality—namely, *How does it feel?* In other words, many times on the journey, objective reality will not seem to mirror spiritual growth, and confusion and doubt will naturally arise. This is usually the result of existing spiritual beliefs that have not yet been cleared.

At this point one must ask of Soul, *This doesn't seem right—how does it feel to you?* In asking this of Soul, you must allow her to answer in her own language—for everything in the Soul center is simpler, including language. Soul may answer that objectively she agrees with God and Spirit that somehow things do not look right. Subjectively though, the situation may *feel* right to her. She will probably be unable to explain in a logical, rational way how this could be so. All Soul can know or intuit is the rightness of the moment. To pressure her to supply a logical rationale for why some illogical situation might be perfect, is to dishonor her, discourage her—and to shut down one's *intuitive* link to existence.

Soul also supplies a moral compass for the journey, tempering the destructive urges of God when He is caught in the anger veil. Soul is most important in the passage from Eden

Consciousness to God Consciousness, and God will be well rewarded for liberating Soul from her veil of pain. Later in the journey, with the value of hindsight, God in His increasing wisdom, can more logically fit together the seemingly illogical puzzle of awakening.

To begin any journey, you must start from where you are. Everyone contains all three centers of consciousness, but one center will seem more prevalent in your life, more comfortable. Whichever center is the most prevalent will tend to be the entry point into the awakening process. For instance, if the primary tone of your life is a heaviness of heart, loneliness, and the need to love and be loved, then you are *Whichever center of consciousness – Soul, Spirit or God - is the most prevalent in your life, that center will tend to be your entry point into the awakening process.* probably spending most of your life in your Soul center. If your thoughts are sentimental and nostalgic, focused on being connected or disconnected, your work will begin with the pain veil. If you are a fearful, anxious person, constantly trying to please others, doing things to earn the approval of others—if your thoughts and feelings are projecting you into an insecure future—if you are aware of postponing the fun of life to gain a more secure future—then you are experiencing life through your Spirit center. The entry point of your journey will be the fear veil.

If you are an angry person, then you are experiencing life through your God center, and your journey will begin with the veil of anger. To begin from the God center is the most difficult and dangerous start. In my own experience, those who are stuck in their God centers rarely awaken. There are many reasons for this, but the most powerful is that blinding beliefs are held by God, and nourished and sustained by the veil of anger. If those beliefs revolve around religion, anything you say or suggest will push the anger button, as though you are attacking God's concept of Himself and of His world. Once God is captured by the anger, nothing will be heard—nothing will penetrate His shield of anger. People who experience life through their God center will always challenge the Master, fighting as though the Master is the enemy. To work with such people is a waste of time and energy, for if God resists the Master's teaching, it becomes the *will* of that individual God to remain asleep. If it is your God's will to remain asleep, then Buddha himself cannot awaken Him.

There is another reason that it so difficult to begin the journey in the God center. His is the most powerful center, where you have the illusion of control, and where fear and pain do not exist. For a God-centered person to think of moving into a place of vulnerability (Soul) or indecisiveness (Sprit) is anathema. Such a shift is simply not likely to happen, unless existence deems it is time for God to return home, and delivers a blow that shatters the false ego center created by anger, plunging the individual suddenly into the other centers and making him aware that he still has a Soul that can hurt and a Spirit that can fear. Otherwise, embarking on a journey with a God who demands total control of His path is generally a path to nowhere … or to the kind of blind ideology that is ravishing creation.

If, however, God has attained partial clarity, where some of the anger veil has been dissolved in this or a previous life, then to begin in God could be the most auspicious. It is all about the veil. The mathematics are simple: more anger, less God; less anger, more God; more anger, less truth, perception, and creativity; less anger, more availability and openness to truth.

Such a God will be able to begin the journey open to the possibility that is the Master's teaching. He will not necessarily totally grasp or understand it, but it will have the ring of truth deep inside. God cannot *know* the truth of it until He is awake, so in the beginning a leap of faith is required. If such a God takes this leap, his success is already assured, for if it is the will of your God that you awaken from the ego

Ego, though powerful, can never be more powerful than the one creating it

nightmare, nothing—no obstacle that ego can put in God's path—can deter Him from ultimate success. Ego, though powerful, can never be more powerful than the one creating it. However, for God to succeed in a balanced awakening, it is imperative that He focus on His children—Soul and Spirit.

Though I have not seen the God center awaken without first laying the foundation of Soul and Spirit awakening, I can imagine the possibility of the phenomenon. It would seem a dangerous awakening, for God would lack the stability and balance provided by the awakening of the Soul and Spirit centers. If successful, the journey would produce a partial enlightenment—one that is very dry, serious and hard—devoid of love and respect, both for self and others. Therefore, it is best to begin the journey with the Soul and Spirit centers where the awakening process is organic and logical, rather than powerful and volatile, as it is in God's awakening. To enter God's awakening with Soul and Spirit awake, is to enter with clarity, balance and stability inside, thereby assuring that your passage through God will be as safe and stable as possible.

As I have noted, to begin the journey, to ignite the process of awakening, contact with someone who has already awakened is naturally best, for even with brief contact an initiation can occur—a subtle, mysterious transmission of light from one center to another. It will be as if a flame has jumped from the awakened one to your very center, reactivating a homing beacon that draws you inward and provides light to guide you home. This is a mysterious transmission, one that is difficult to describe, but for the journey home, it is an invaluable gift. Absent this possibility, you must ignite the process on your own. To do this, clear intent is essential, so you must first be in right frame of mind. Spend time contemplating the journey. Fears will naturally arise, as will sadness, as Soul contemplates what might be lost, not to mention God's angst, for implicit in undertaking the journey is recognition that the way He has structured and controlled your life has failed. Admitting failure is not His strong point.

Expect your three centers of consciousness to experience periods of doubt and indecision as they contemplate undertaking the journey. Wait until there seems to be consensus inside—until you thoroughly understand that life as you are living it is not working for you. Wait for the moment of clarity when all parts of you seem to be in agreement, when you are ready to leap into the unknown. In that moment, when your consciousness seems most unified and focused, send your clear intent to existence that you are ready to awaken, to begin the journey home. Do this in any way that feels right to you. Direct your intent to existence, the universe, to God, to a Goddess, to your higher power—however you conceptualize that elusive mystery, that something *out there*. Once you have delivered clear intent to journey home, your journey has begun. Now you must be alert, and trust whatever higher power you believe in, for trust will now become all important.

No one likes to be in fear or pain, but to live in the ego world is to periodically be in these states. All the time that you are hurting, the ego is being nourished, feeding off of your life. Every time you are in fear, ego is feeding.

No one likes to be in fear or pain, but to live in the ego world is to periodically be in these states.

Every time you are in anger, ego feasts. Just as fear and pain are givens in the ego experience, so too are all the patterns used to control, distance, and distract you from what you are experiencing. Yet to clear these veils, you must be *in* them. Hence, the first paradox encountered on your journey. In awakening, you will experience things becoming worse before getting better. The reason for this relates to the first two veils— pain and fear. The ego is constantly directing your awareness away from the veils. To do so looks logical, for no one wants to be in fear or pain. But what existence does is hit your pain and fear buttons, and this is perceived as being very punishing. You ask yourself—*I am a spiritual person desirous of moving into the light, so why is existence being so hard on me?*

The answer is simple. You cannot clear a veil when your awareness is constantly distracted elsewhere—usually to the tapes playing in your head, where you hear fear and pain replaying their tales of woe. So if you feel that existence is being hard on you, you must instead become aware of the *reality* of what is occurring. That reality is a very uncomfortable physical sensation in area of the heart (Soul, which experiences pain) or the *solar plexus* (Spirit, which experiences fear). Existence will tend to trigger the fear and pain buttons until each sensation is strong enough for you to notice. Remember, all the power of ego, all the power of your past, will be distracting you on your journey, trying to get you lost in the familiar pain and fear messages that you've heard all of your life.

Existence is not punishing you—it is trying to make you aware of intense physical sensations. Period. Without becoming aware of these sensations, you have no hope of clearing them. Once you have become aware of the pain as a physical sensation, the fear as physical sensation, then you are ready to begin the meditation that will clear the pain and fear veils. Each time a pain or fear button is pushed, be alert. Instantly you will be drawn into your head, where you will get lost, as always. But something new will begin to occur—a voice will tell you that you are experiencing an uncomfortable sensation, and you will be drawn to the bodily sensation. Do not fight the sensation, or try to control it. The objective is to withdraw your energy from it, and to fight or attempt to control the sensation is to connect to it. Both strategies will be supported by the ego. Instead, detach from the sensation, and watch for as long as you can.

Beginning is the hardest part. At first you may be able to watch for only a few seconds before getting lost again in the ego tapes playing in your head. *You don't get it. You aren't doing it right. You aren't good enough. It won't work.* Endless messages to distract and discourage you. Then a voice will remind you that you are simply watching a sensation, and your awareness will be

Once you master the meditation – that is, once you become adept at seeing the sensation as being separate from yourself and can separate at will from it - you will find yourself able to watch it anywhere, for any length of time, whenever the veils are triggered.

drawn back to reality—an uncomfortable, *physical* reality. This time you will be able to watch a little longer before slipping back into your head—and once again, a voice will remind you of the sensation. Each time you return to your vigil, you will be able to watch the sensation for a longer period before being distracted. Do not get discouraged, for with practice, you will become adept at this meditation.

It is best to begin the meditation sitting alone—comfortable, quiet, and with as few distractions as possible. Once you master the meditation—that is, once you become adept at seeing the sensation as being separate from yourself and can separate at will from it—you will find yourself able to watch it anywhere, for any length of time, whenever the veils are triggered. As an adept, you will be able to start clearing a sensation the moment any veil is triggered—the moment your fear or pain buttons are pushed. The most auspicious time for meditating is at night, when you can clear many layers of a veil. I refer to those nights when you lie awake gripped by fear or pain. If you have such nights, you know from experience that you will not get much sleep, so begin your meditation and watch as layer after layer of the veils dissolve.

Once you enter the veils and begin to clear them, you will notice a few things. First, the sensation will intensify as you watch it, then will abate, then will begin to intensify again. This is because the veils are layered. As you move into a layer, the sensation will intensify. As you move through it, the sensation will begin to abate. As you move into the next layer, the sensation will again intensify. If you find that you need to stop the meditation, always stop between layers, when the sensation seems to have abated. Unless it is absolutely necessary, do not stop when the sensation is at its most intense. If you do, you will be in the intensity for hours, and it will be most uncomfortable.

You will also notice that the sensations seem to move within the area that you are watching, and that they also move from veil to veil. In other words, if you watch the pain sensation around your heart area, you will find the sensation moving to fear, which is in the stomach area. Once you are in the process of awakening, the sensations will move back and forth between these two centers for they must be cleared together. You cannot awaken Soul without also awakening Spirit, for Spirit must be ready to take care of Soul once she is back.

The sensations will change many times as you penetrate and clear the veils. They can become very intense, particularly around the heart, varying from a sharp pain to a dull heavy sensation. Many experience a place in the pain veil where the sensation feels almost like a knife plunged into the heart. I only wish to inform and prepare you that some of these sensations—particularly those deep in the veils, can be very intense. After you become familiar with the meditation, you will develop an intuitive knowledge of which sensations are caused by the veils, and which are physical sensations that may indicate a condition requiring medical attention. Always trust your awareness—it will inevitably be drawn to the sensation that needs to be watched, even as ego tries to confuse or distract you.

Once you enter the veils and begin processing through meditation, it is best to continue clearing till there are no more sensations emerging. If you stop meditating before the veils are cleared, you will thereafter feel as if you are living closer to them, experiencing pain and fear more intensely.

Remember—when it comes to clearing the veils, "Once begun, best to finish".

This is because once you begin the process of clearing the veils, you become more aware of them, and thus they become more accessible. Remember—when it comes to clearing the veils, "Once begun, best to finish".

How long will it take to clear these veils? It depends

on several variables. How determined are you to end your suffering? How attached are you to your pain and fear? Ultimately, the process of awakening is an interaction between you and your determination to be free, and Existence—which will, in its mysterious inimitable way, lead you home. You may be impatient, determined to awaken swiftly. Nevertheless, Existence may set a slower pace, for the faster the awakening, the more intense the experience. When it comes to awakening, Existence will have her way. When you complete your journey and look back on it, you will see that she did know best, and that your awakening unfolded perfectly *for you*.

Some clear the fear and pain veils in a matter of a few months of entering them. These people have both determination and minimal obligations in the material world. They also have appropriate guidance. Such people enter the veils and do not stop clearing until the process is complete. Though they complete the process remarkably fast, these months are also very dark. For these veils are the very essence of ego darkness, and to move in and through them so quickly is to move through the very heart of darkness with only faith and trust that there is light at the end of the tunnel.

Some take years to clear the first two veils. These people usually have families that require expending energy and responsibility. Existence moves these people through the veils more slowly, marshaling the human energy and wherewithal that it takes to simultaneously tend to responsibilities in the world and to awaken.

Nevertheless, with sufficient motivation and the support of

Existence, one should be able to clear the majority of the pain and fear veils within a year. This is a very individual journey, and while I hesitate to put a timeline to it, I also want to convey the possibility that you can clear your pain and fear forever in a relatively short period of time.

Once through these two veils you enter a new world, the world of Eden Consciousness. Before this point you will always have doubts. You will ask yourself: *Is this path real? Am I getting anywhere? Have I been tricked?* Only after clearing the fear and pain veils will you know that something real has happened—that something fundamental has changed. You are in a new world, and there is no going back. Nor will you want to. You will feel a new sensitivity and innocence that will vary in intensity, depending on whether your passage through the veils was rapid or slow. If it was rapid and intense, Existence will give you a breather so you can adjust to the newness. In clearing these two veils, light or consciousness has been liberated. Time will be required to stabilize this new consciousness, and to experience and explore its nature.

If another person does not feel good to her, Soul will automatically disappear, to be instantly replaced by the more detached Spirit, who offers her a natural protection from the toxic energy emitted by the ego

Though two parts of you will have returned to a state of innocence—innocent love (Soul), and innocent trust (Spirit)—you will awaken into a world still shrouded in darkness, one that neither recognizes nor understands innocence. Liberated Souls and Spirits that no longer march to the drumbeat of *should* perplex and exasperate those still in ego darkness. Soul, no longer compelled to connect to people out of a sense of *should*, begins to connect when it feels right to do so. If another person does not feel good to her, Soul will automatically disappear, to be instantly replaced by the more detached Spirit, who offers her a natural protection from the toxic energy emitted by the ego.

To some, with whom Soul previously connected, she will now be absent if their energy is toxic. If the ego energy is too toxic, Soul will be *unable* to be present to it, and if she is not there it is impossible for love and caring to be there. Without the ego veils it becomes increasingly difficult to even pretend, for false ego masks and patterns dissolve with the veils. Quite simply, if the environment is not nurturing and supportive for Soul, she will not be there. Spirit will be there, and his quality of detachment will offer protection as you move through the world.

You might think that awakening puts you in a perilous position—innocence in a world of sharks—but it is not what ego fear would have you imagine. For one thing, even though you have returned to innocence, more loving and trusting than you have been since childhood, you are still an adult, with enough adult experience to enable you to navigate in the world. There is also an increasing presence of God in your life, and God is anything but innocent. For with the safe deliverance of His children—Soul and Spirit—God, if he has not already done so, begins to appear. As He must, He begins to awaken and protect his creations, and take his rightful place in the world.

Once stabilized in Eden Consciousness, you will begin to move to the next state, which is God Consciousness. In this state, God has awakened from the ancient veil of anger and is conscious of who He really is. He is God. The God center is so powerful and volatile that you will need the clear and stable foundation of an awakened Soul and Spirit to move through this stage safely. Once awakened, these two centers provide the clarity and stability that enables God to awaken from His ancient nightmare of anger, jealousy and revenge with a minimum of damage to Himself and others. Caught in the anger veil, there are no limits to His imaginings of malice. You may notice in the anger veil that you have outrageous fantasies of perfect revenge, or of greatness and grandeur. At times these fantasies are alternately abhorrent to Soul and scary to Spirit. These feelings go to the very nature of God. He contains all potentiality—hence there is no end to His imagination. It is a testament to His essential goodness that most of His angry imaginings go unfulfilled.

In some people God is hidden behind a mask of equanimity. For those with such a hidden God, after reaching Eden Consciousness, He begins to appear. After enjoying the clarity, peace and gentleness of the awakened Soul, it will be a shock to have the angry one suddenly begin appearing. For those who are in denial of their anger—of their God center—it is shocking to discover not only the anger hidden inside, but also the depth of it. They will feel enlightened one moment, and plunged into the ugly darkness of the anger veil the next moment. There will be an intense contrast between the clarity and delight of the liberated Spirit and Soul centers, and the darkness of the anger veil in the God center. If your God is hidden, however disquieting it is to find yourself moving in and out of anger, such an experience is both timely and necessary.

For those who are in denial of their anger – of their God center – it is shocking to discover not only the anger hidden inside, but also the depth of it.

Having awakened Soul and Spirit and reclaimed peace and harmony, you will not want your new state disturbed—and God is a great disturbance. Yet, however disturbing, whenever God appears is the perfect time for you. However much you may resist, it will be time to clear the anger veil, and like the two that preceded it, you cannot clear the anger veil without being *in* it. So with the emergence of God you will find your God flaring into anger.

Now you begin the passage from Eden Consciousness to God Consciousness. The anger veil is cleared differently than the Soul and Spirit veils, for the God center is located in the third eye, in the area of the forehead, and there is no sensation to watch. The toxicity of the anger veil produces a sensation, but it tends to follow, rather than accompany episodes of anger. The sensations produced by the anger veil are headaches, and if you spend a lot of time in your angry God center, you will experience them often. In your passage through God, expect headaches following episodes of anger. Though there is no sensation to watch during this passage, the technique of detaching from the anger veil—withholding light and energy from it—remains the same.

Without a physical sensation to focus on and detach from, how does God clear this veil? You must remember two things. First, He is God, with all that this implies. Second, two parts of God, Soul and Spirit, are clear and awake at this point— and though they have been held in conflict and separation for so long, they have always been part of the one God. While God may be blinded in His third eye by anger, He can still see clearly through two eyes—no longer blinded by pain (the veil surrounding Soul) or fear (the veil surrounding Spirit). This is the key to the awakening of God.

When God begins awakening He will appear more frequently, angry and blaming within and without, according to the familiar patterning of your own inner God. Initially He is blinded and deafened by anger, as He has always been. But then something new begins to appear.

When God stops nourishing the anger veil, it dies.

It will seem as if He is caught in the anger one moment, and the next moment as if He is standing outside of Himself, witnessing Himself caught in the anger. When God is simultaneously caught in anger and witnessing Himself, it is the beginning of the end of the anger veil, for every moment He is separate from and witnessing the anger, he is detached from the veil. His light is withdrawn from the veil. At this point, like the pain and fear veils, the anger veil begins dissolving layer by layer. The key with the anger veil is awareness. As God becomes aware of how ugly anger makes Him look, sound, think and feel, the less attached He will be to it. The more He separates from it, the less light and energy it receives from Him. When God stops nourishing the anger veil, it dies.

The passage through God tends to be lengthy for several reasons. The anger veil is more ancient than the pain and fear veils. It also leads into the final veil, the mother or serpent veil. The serpent veil begins to appear about halfway through the process of clearing the anger veil. As God awakens, He becomes aware of this final veil. At this point you will find yourself clearing two veils in tandem. One is masculine (anger), and one is feminine (*other*—or serpent). The clearing of both veils simultaneously is the second alchemical marriage—the merging and harmonizing of masculine and feminine—of God and Existence.

Through this difficult passage you will find that the trust liberated from the fear veil not only serves you well, but deepens as God's illusionary control over life dissolves with the veil of anger. More and more God is called to trust in Existence for His deliverance. With growing awareness He sees the true nature of the anger—its mindlessness, cruelty and deceptiveness. And yet, not being fully awake, not yet back on His throne, He worries what life will be like without this ancient advisor. Without anger, where will be His passion? Without anger, how will He function? The answer is that He will function better than ever—but during the dark passage, He will not know this. All He will have to keep Him on course is the trust that will both deepen and strengthen.

Alas—poor Soul, newly liberated, sensitive, tender and delicate, seems to disappear with the awakening of God. It is one of the hallmarks of this passage, that having reclaimed

Soul, you seem to lose her again. During this passage you will develop a deep appreciation of her, and will long for her to return. But when anger is present, the energy is far too toxic for Soul to be present. So during much of the awakening of God, do not expect to see much of her. Not to worry—she will be waiting at the end of the dark tunnel to welcome God with a loving embrace.

Do not be surprised to find yourself surrounded by other angry Gods during this passage, for whom better to trigger an angry God than another angry God? Remember, in order to clear a veil, you must be in it, and *If your God has been hiding inside, He will now* as with previous *appear to protect the newly awakened twins.* veils, your whole ego experience is to deny, repress, or express "appropriately" the ugliness that is the veil. This passage is especially troubling to spiritual people, particularly if their spiritual belief systems affirm the qualities of Soul (love and gentleness) and Spirit (fairness and good works). The result will be denial of anger, which is denial of God. Such people tend to find angry Gods appearing in their midst to provoke the ugliness hidden within them.

If your God has been hiding inside, He will now appear to protect the newly awakened twins. Naturally, He will be angry and blaming towards existence as if existence is once again working against Him—when in truth it is working for Him. Existence does not want God to be angry, for anger is destructive and toxic to life *and* existence. It is toxic when it is expressed, and toxic when it is repressed. Existence is merely provoking God to appear from His hiding place to confront His anger—to see what it is doing, to take responsibility for it, and to clear it. Only by doing this can God end the 'blame game' forever.

As you move through this passage, you will find yourself having to throw anger on others. Every moment God is captured by the veil, he is generating toxicity which builds up inside and must eventually be released. Meanwhile, ego is pointing the finger of blame, goading and urging God to release it on this one or that one. All will be perfectly justified—for before God releases such ugliness on another, He will have to be convinced by the anger that doing so is justified—that is, why the other 'deserves it'. So if you find yourself throwing anger on another, who better to spar with but another angry God?

There is no *right* way to get through this passage. But one way or another, existence will trigger the anger at the perfect moment in the perfect way for you. God's pride will be bruised moving through this passage, but with luck, in the end His dignity will remain intact.

Another experience to be aware of in this passage is the sense of aloneness. Aloneness is different from loneliness.

Loneliness concerns your relationship with others. Aloneness concerns your relationship with Existence.

Loneliness is part of Soul's passage. With the clearing of the pain and fear veils, the reuniting of Soul with Spirit that occurs when the veils are cleared, loneliness—the need for some 'other'—disappears. The neediness, the loneliness of Soul disappears—for she is no longer alone, needing another to feel complete. She is whole. However, when you are in your God center, particularly in reference to relationships, you feel that you need no one. God is the place where we feel completely self-sufficient. Loneliness concerns your relationship with others. Aloneness concerns your relationship with Existence. In the passage through God's awakening, you cannot escape the aloneness of God.

While the passage through the pain and fear veils seems mechanical, watching layer after layer of uncomfortable sensations, the passage through the anger veil is more like an awakening. It is God awakening from a long dark night of sleep that has been punctuated by fitful dreams. Now He is slowly coming back to His senses and sanity.

There is a place in God's awakening where the cosmic joke is revealed. This is a place where enough of the anger is dissolved, where enough of God is once again conscious— where in an instant God realizes who He is. He *knows* rather than *believes* He is God. In that instant, looking into the world clearly for the first time in ages, He sees Himself reflected everywhere. Not only is He God, there is nothing but God in visible creation. He is everywhere, and the special-ness that was God, the belief of God, disappears in an instant of knowing. For if everything is God, *everyone* is God, then there is nothing special about Him. He becomes as ordinary as a grain of sand. Everything He searched for He already was. The cosmic game of hide and seek is revealed for what it is. The punch line has been delivered and is understood. There will still be anger at this point, but with this realization God has regained his throne and it is just a matter of time before the remaining anger of the veil will be cleared.

Once God is awake enough to know who He is, it is time to focus on the final veil, the veil of the mother—the serpent veil. This final veil is very subtle and mysterious. Like the pain and fear veils, the serpent veil creates a sensation in the physical body. It is a very subtle, deep sensation.

Once God is awake enough to know who He is, it is time to focus on the final veil, the veil of the mother – the serpent veil.

Begin to look for it when your anger is triggered. Look in the area across the chest—the breast area. It is a sensation of irritability. This is easier for women than men to detect. Women who experience PMS experience their consciousness slipping into the mother veil—a place where they become irritable, and sensitive to people, energy, vibration, noise, and even light. This experience transcends the physical consequences of pre-menstrual hormonal fluctuations. At its deepest and darkest, you will feel venomous—hence I call this the serpent veil, for the serpent seems to be the perfect symbol for its mysterious unpredictable nature.

For men, this is a difficult veil to detect. It is a feminine veil, and as such is part of the ego denial of the feminine in most males. To find it requires alertness and effort. Just as the Soul and Spirit veils seem connected, one triggering the other, so too the Father and Mother veils are connected. The difference, particularly for those living in more masculine cultures where the mother / feminine is denied, is that Westerners are much more comfortable in the masculine veil of anger—for in the anger, however crazy it makes you, it nonetheless gives the comforting illusion that someone or something is to blame. That is, no matter how irrational you become in anger, the anger offers a logical, rational reason for your anger.

Not so with the mother / serpent veil. The ego developed in the West being masculine, deludes itself that it is logical and rational, even when it is obviously not. Unlike the feminine pain veil, which is *The mother / serpent veil separates you* apparent to people of *(Soul – Spirit - God) from Existence - the* both sexes, the feminine *mother goddess ocean of consciousness.* mother veil is not. It is the deepest and most hidden veil. Unlike other veils, it does not define a center. In other words the mother veil, the veil of the goddess, does not contain a mother or goddess behind it. It does not define a center. Rather, it defines a circumference (Illustration I). The mother / serpent veil separates you (Soul—Spirit—God) from Existence—the mother goddess ocean of consciousness.

Unlike the other veils, which are easily recognizable and labeled—who could not recognize pain, fear or anger—the mother veil has no such clear or defined label or attribute. As I mentioned, this veil produces a physical sensation and requires detached watching to clear it. By the time God becomes aware of it, He is also sufficiently clear to watch it, and it does require the power of God to clear it. Spirit and/ or God can clear the fear and pain veils, but only the power of God can clear the mother veil.

When the anger veil is triggered, and God is sufficiently awake to not be distracted by where the anger is pointing, He should begin to look across the breast area for a deep subtle sensation of irritability. Once found, do not let go of it. Watch it closely, for it will move and seemingly change form. It appears to be dull, not sharp like the sensations of pain and fear.

Entering the veil you experience a feeling of irritability. But as you move deeper, this sensation can become dull and heavy—a feeling of heaviness that didn't entirely lift with the clearing of the pain veil.

Unlike the other veils, which are easily recognizable and labeled – who could not recognize pain, fear or anger – the mother veil has no such clear or defined label or attribute.

At times it will seem as though you missed part of the pain veil. This will not be pain—it will be more the fragrance of pain than pain itself. At times the sensation will remind you of the fear veil. This will not be fear—it will be more the fragrance of fear than fear itself. For this is the mother veil—the mother of all veils, and it contains within it, the seeds of the other veils. When you wonder if you are encountering parts of the fear and pain veils that were missed, you are not. You are encountering the seeds of the pain and fear veils.

The sensation will initially move across the breast area. At times it will seem to deepen, as though you are following roots that are spiraling deep inside. Keep watching. At other times, it will seem to move up or down in the center of the chest. Keep watching. This veil comes and goes in waves, like the pain and fear veils. As you clear it you become familiar with it, and God discovers something curious. Before He erupts in anger, He will first experience the sensation that another veil is present.

Unbeknownst to Him, before the anger veil is triggered, the mother / serpent veil has already been triggered, and to be aware of the mother veil and watch it when it appears, is to further weaken and undermine the power of the anger veil over God.

God is now working at the deepest level, in the birthplace of anger. The mother /serpent veil is a grueling, tedious, mysterious veil. All God needs to do is stay alert, and watch it when it is present. As He watches this veil, more and more anger will dissipate. When anger does appear, it does not linger like before, but disappears suddenly, leaving God laughing at the ridiculousness of it. Though anger is still present, it no longer controls or possesses Him. The king has returned to his throne.

By the time you encounter the serpent veil, you are basically awake and in God consciousness. While perhaps not complete, a process of integration of Soul, Spirit and God will be occurring, and can be assisted by asking yourself the following questions: "Do I trust the God within? Do I love the God within?" These questions will trigger Spirit's awareness that he might still be trusting outside gods, rather than the God within. They will trigger Soul's awareness that the God within, who has blamed her for so long, is now transformed. Her love now automatically flows towards Him, facilitating the Soul's integration back into God, even as Spirit's trust re-integrates him back into God.

As this final veil of separation appears, it will basically be one God, one unified consciousness that begins to perceive it. In the East, this place on the journey is called *samadhi with seed*. You are awake, there is still a subtle sense of "I", and bliss and peace remain elusive. You are awake, with the seed of the ego illusion remaining to be cleared. One can get stuck here, for you are awake, and know it. But if you remain here, you will find yourself subject to occasional flare-ups of anger, as well as continuing disturbances to your peace, seemingly coming from others.

In clearing this veil, as in clearing all the veils, expect to be discouraged at times, for the process will seem endless. It is not. Know that you are close to the end when the sensation becomes focused in the center of your chest, no longer moving about up and down. Then you are close. Just keep watching.

10. Meditations

This chapter is devoted to the meditation technique that I have referred to throughout the book. This technique does not require concentration, contemplation or control. It simply requires a focused awareness.

What is focused awareness? Every time you are *This technique does not require concentration, contemplation or control. It simply requires a focused awareness.* confronted with a problem or challenge, you automatically and effortlessly focus your awareness on it. Here, the veils are your problem, and they are unlike any problem you have encountered before. Because they are so challenging, the Awakening meditation does require effort, particularly in the beginning. As I have explained, the veils distract your awareness, moving your focus to the illusions the veils are generating. Your challenge, especially in the beginning, is to ignore these illusions and learn to continuously re-focus your awareness on the veils—on the physical sensations they create as they transform light into darkness and consciousness into *un*-consciousness.

The beginning of the meditation is the most difficult, for ego will continue to do what it has always done. Ego will distract you from the reality of what is happening—a sensation in the physical body—to the illusion that it is creating in your mind. But once you have developed the ability to focus and *watch* the sensations, you will be able to do the meditation anywhere. You will be able to call upon this ability whenever you find yourself in a hurting or sad state, or in a fearful or anxious state.

One   Find a quiet space free of distractions.

Two   Sit comfortably.

Three Close your eyes.

Four   Ask yourself, "What am I feeling?" In other words, ask yourself if you are feeling hurt-sad-depressed, or fearful-anxious-panicky. Since one can't *feel* a label, and yet you are obviously feeling something, ask yourself what it is you are actually feeling. Where is the physical sensation you are feeling that the mind is labeling sad-painful or anxious-fearful? Look around your heart area for the pain sensation. Look around the stomach area for the fear sensation. Do not look for something unusual, for these sensations have always been there. Look for the obvious. Trust your awareness, for it will usually focus on exactly where you need to watch.

Five   Once you have located the physical sensation, detach your awareness from it and, like a scientist, simply observe it as a physical phenomenon, neither for nor against. It is simply an uncomfortable physical sensation. Do not try to control or fight it. Do not try to understand it or fathom the illusionary message or teaching that it holds for you, for to do so will simply take you back into your mind, where you will spin your wheels as you have always done in the past. Keep reminding yourself that it is only a physical sensation, one that means nothing and has nothing to teach you.

Six The power of the ego distraction will pull you back into your mind, back into the familiar nightmare. You will have a thought or a remembrance that you were observing a sensation. Detach and watch. In the beginning it will probably be difficult to hold the awareness on the sensation for more than a few minutes before getting distracted by the fearful, hurtful thoughts in your mind. You may even have thoughts that you cannot do the meditation—that you are not advanced enough or good enough. You may have thoughts that the meditation is not working, or that it won't work.

Treat these thoughts like the distractions they are, and bring your awareness back to the sensation. Watch until you once again find yourself distracted by familiar negative thinking, and simply shift your awareness back to reality—a very uncomfortable physical sensation. Each time you return to the sensation, you will find yourself able to watch it for a longer period before once again finding yourself distracted.

Seven Once you are able to watch sensations for extended periods of five, ten or fifteen minutes without getting distracted, you will begin to notice that the sensations come in waves. This wavelike quality may be subtle at first, then become intense, then may abate somewhat, only to intensify once again. As I pointed out elsewhere, the veils are layered, and as you move into each layer, sensations will begin to intensify then abate, only to intensify again as you clear layer after layer.

Sometimes the sensation will seem to disappear. If it does, you may stop the meditation for that sitting. If, however, you have the time and determination to continue watching, you can self-activate the sensation by simply imagining a familiar painful or fearful situation. This will be enough to re-ignite the sensation.

Though not always possible, it is best to end the meditation between layers, when the sensation, while not entirely gone, is nonetheless not intense.

The ego does not want you to do this meditation. The whole purpose of the meditation is to cut the flow of nourishment to ego's roots, the place it protects most because it is the place of its greatest vulnerability. In addition to the familiar distractions of painful / fearful thoughts, new thoughts will be generated— thoughts about the meditation itself. *It is not working. I cannot do it. I am not doing it right. It is too hard. If it were working, why am I still having waves of sensations?* These messages will be endless. The sensations themselves will seem endless. Remind yourself, especially when you become discouraged, that you can be aware of either the sensation *or* the nightmare being generated by it. In either case, the sensation will be there. The only difference is that by *watching*, you are dissolving the sensation, whereas when you are lost in the familiar ego nightmare, you are perpetuating it.

Since you are going to be in discomfort from the sensation anyway, you might as well settle in and watch. You have probably endured far greater discomfort in pursuit of worldly goals, goals that proved ephemeral. Remember that you are now engaged in reclaiming your Soul and Spirit. Watching the veils may seem endless, but it is not. Continue watching until the sensations begin to disappear, the veils are clear, and innocent Soul and Spirit are once again bathed in light.

There is another meditation that will arise *spontaneously* as the veils are cleared, but for you intrepid Souls and Spirits, anxious to end the ego nightmare and reclaim your lives, I will include it here.

Eight This meditation is simple, to be done wherever you think of it when you are in situations interacting with others. It is a simple awareness of the false ego mask, the false patterning of ego existence.

Whenever it occurs to you, simply ask yourself, *"Am I being true in this moment, or false?"* By asking this question, there will be a subtle detachment from the falseness of the mask that you are wearing at the moment—an awareness that your speech or actions are not flowing spontaneously—that you are, in effect, pretending to be someone rather than spontaneously being who you are.

Be careful not to judge what you see, or change whatever pattern or mask you become aware of. Rather, make the neutral observation that in that moment you feel phony or forced, that you are not being who or what you really are. Again, make no judgments as to whether this is right or wrong. Make no attempt to alter your behavior or try to be more real, authentic or sincere.

Each time you find yourself in this false pattern or mask, it will appear successively clearer, in sharper focus. With no effort on your part, the patterning creating the mask will begin to dissolve, as your energy is naturally, effortlessly withdrawn. You have seen the ego pretense of you.

This meditation will work in tandem with the watching meditation, enabling the awareness to move through outer layers of ego patterning, towards the centers, even as you are working to liberate the centers themselves. As you work with this meditation, you can even affirm yourself, priding yourself on how cleverly you fooled others with your false mask. This is alright, since the purpose of the meditation is to tell yourself the truth—to become aware of what is. How you handle what you see, vis-a-vis others, is entirely up to you. You are, after all, a living albeit sleeping God. Most people are used to, and more comfortable with, a false mask than with the truth. Once you have awakened, you will have plenty of time and opportunity to both be your truth, and assume false masks when it suits you.

11. The Journey Home

In the previous chapter I have focused on the mechanics of the awakening process. Now I will focus on how it feels to wake up—what you will experience internally as the centers awaken.

Unlike modalities that promise a quick fix but fail to provide one, the awakening process will not appeal to your ego. Ego, the false one, forever alien to God's creation, wants to continue to exist. It seeks to be healed, in order to become more functional in an

The veils are the source of all problems. Remove them and you uncover the perfection that you already are.

increasingly dysfunctional world. But ego is detached from reality. It continues to promise that in some illusionary future, through some self-help program or miracle of medicine, you will become happy and secure. Of course this future never comes, and unfulfilled promises become more promises, always to be fulfilled in that elusive future.

The reality is, you are already enlightened. You have always been enlightened, in your centers. The awakening process does not promise to make the ego experience happy and fulfilling. That is impossible. Instead, it teaches you how to remove what is obscuring and separating you from what already exists—your inherent perfection, and enlightenment.

The veils are the source of all problems. Remove them and you uncover the perfection that you already are. Perfection is unique to each individual—each being a unique flower in the garden. I cannot describe what this flower will look like. I can only teach you how to remove the false weeds that hide the true *you*.

Once you begin processing the veils, your internal experience of life starts to change dramatically, even though your outer life will at first appear the same. More energy will move inward to support your awakening, and as you progress, you may find yourself working to balance your inner needs with your responsibilities in the world. As the inner world opens to you, you may find that some worldly activities will begin to seem boring. When your inner world becomes more interesting and real to you than the outside world, these activities will drop very naturally from your life. The key to any of these changes is that you allow them to occur naturally. Do not force anything. Change must happen as a result of your evolving consciousness, rather than as a result of your imposing a condition of *should* on the process. Allow as much as possible for life to be as it *is*, rather than as you were taught it *should* be. This will help you to focus on the reality of *now*.

Once you have entered and begun processing the veils, it will seem at times that they are constantly there. They *are* constantly there, and they always have been. The only difference is that you now understand what ego was hiding from you—what ego was distracting you from. Having entered the fear and pain veils, it is imperative to remember 'it is only a sensation, an uncomfortable physical sensation'. In watching the sensation you detach not only from it, but from the fearful or painful thoughts being generated by it. The inner experience is now one of feeling that existence is being hard on you, punishing you. But if you reflect, you will see that whatever fear or pain state you now find yourself in, is nearly identical to what you have experienced all your life. The difference is that instead of using your energy to run from the reality of what you are feeling, you are confronting it, clearing it, and reclaiming your life from it.

Clearing the fear and pain veils is the most difficult passage of awakening, for until they have been processed, you will have no clear centers from which to look. All is dark, illusion within illusion. Trust and faith are what will see you through this first and most important passage. There will be difficulties and challenges to follow, but with the awakening of Soul and Spirit, you not only begin to see clearly, you will begin to *know*.

Parts of the inner you have been through many experiences over the course of lifetimes, and once the ego darkness of the veils is dissolved, these parts of you will begin to remember, and to know certain transcendent truths.

Parts of the inner you have been through many experiences over the course of lifetimes, and once the ego darkness of the veils is dissolved, these parts of you will begin to remember, and to *know* certain transcendent truths. You will be amazed at what will emerge into consciousness—things you simply *know*, and know absolutely. It will initially startle you that you could know such things, and with such certainty—things that you haven't studied, memorized, or been examined on. You may feel unworthy, as if you have no right to know what you now do—that you do not have the credentials which are the requirement of knowledge in the ego world. And yet, you now *know* that certain things are true.

As your awakening proceeds, you will become familiar and comfortable with these *knowings* that are percolating into consciousness—many times mysteriously appearing at the exact time you need them. What begins as something mysterious,

As you move into the awakening process, more and more you will speak your truth. And then you will better understand what I mean when I say that most people do not want to hear it.

and to many as something disconcerting, will become familiar and commonplace. It makes sense. Everything that has ever been known by your God or other Gods is hidden in consciousness, under layers of ego confusion and darkness. Remove the confusing darkness, and what was once known, again becomes available. In fact, as these *knowings* begin to appear, you may experience a simultaneous feeling that 'I have always known this'. You are correct, for whatever is known was always known, simply forgotten in the ego sleep.

Perhaps you will become increasingly aware of the falseness of ego—of the falseness of *you*. Ego has been telling you that life is wonderful, even though your marriage may be falling apart, or your child may be taking drugs. Instead of accepting what ego has been saying, and what you have been parroting to others, you will become aware of the falseness—not only of your words, but of the false façade that is your life. You will become more truthful as you awaken. Though this is inevitable, you may find it more convenient to give the lie that others expect, for you must still live and function in the ego world, where truth is the last thing people want to hear. The importance to you in terms of your awakening, is that now you know it is a lie—a falseness. Though I am not trying to condone lying, I am giving you permission to make a difficult path as easy as possible. As you move into the awakening process, more and more you will speak your truth. And then you will better understand what I mean when I say that most people do not want to hear it. By then though, you will be strong and wise enough to understand.

In the beginning, it is enough to recognize that the façade of falseness is the ego structure. Be aware of it. To recognize the falseness does not require you to change it. To see it is enough, for once you begin to see the false patterns, your energy will automatically start to withdraw, and these patterns will begin to dissolve. If you struggle to *fix* the ego patterns you will waste your energy, for you will only create new and more sophisticated patterns that will have to be cleared later on. To work through the ego structure and patterns you must move inward, becoming aware of layer after layer of falseness and clearing each one. In doing so you move your awareness, your light, towards your center, and the true *you*. The ego structure has no center. There is no *there* there. What passes for centers in the ego are simply constellations of patterning. A button is pushed, and a predictable response is automatically triggered. After you have awakened, each unique moment elicits a unique response. Ego cannot exist in the moment—therefore, each unique moment elicits a patterned response that is completely disconnected from the reality of the moment.

As your awareness of the false ego façade grows, you may find yourself slipping into a sort of spiritual crisis. The person you thought you were, is revealed as false. Inevitably, you will ask yourself—"Who am I?"   During the awakening process, you are the one who is separating from, observing, and becoming aware of the false ego facade and patterns. The ego structure is inherently unstable, and seems to become more so as you awaken—particularly after you begin dissolving the veils, from which it gets its strength. Under stress, the false ego centers will begin to fail, drawing you into earlier and less sophisticated ego patterns. As you struggle to return from these early ego patterns to an adult, more sophisticated ego layer, you may feel at times as if you are 'losing it". I am describing a state you already know—cycling between adult and childish behaviors. The only difference as you awaken will be your growing awareness of the falseness of all the ego layers that you encounter, and your growing strength and wisdom as the light of consciousness is returned to you.

With this growing awareness, the old patterns will begin to dissolve. Recognized for what they are, your support of these patterns will be automatically withdrawn—no effort required. You cease to support what is making your life miserable. As you move inward from the periphery, you will come closer not only to your true centers, but also to the veils surrounding them. Inevitably, you will start being pulled into the veils themselves. Be alert. If you begin to feel depressed or panicky, it is time to process the veils. Find the physical sensations, detach and watch them, and dissolve the veils by withholding your energy from them. Once you begin processing the veils, you will be working to dissolve ego from the center as well as from the periphery. Using the analogy of a noxious weed, you will be withholding nourishment from the roots, even as you hack away at the plant growing from them.

At times you may wonder if you are going mad. That has already happened, for ego is the only madness within you. The difference is one of intensity, for as you awaken and experience the ego thought and behavior patterns, you experience them more intensely. The reason for this is that the entire ego,

The more complex and sophisticated ego is, the more mechanical and dead you will feel, for all your aliveness is being consumed to support your ego.

from its roots (the veils) to its structure (the patterns) requires energy to support, sustain, and give it the *appearance* of life. It is basically dead. The more complex and sophisticated ego is, the more mechanical and dead you will feel, for all your *aliveness* is being consumed to support your ego. As you awaken—as ego dissolves—consciousness or light is freed up and returned to you, the one who is now aware. During the awakening process, the light or consciousness that is *you*, increases in strength and intensity, enabling you to see more, and more clearly.

It is the difference between shining a flashlight first with weak batteries and then with strong batteries into a dark room. With weak batteries, objects in the room are visible, but not clear. Colors appear grey and flat rather than bright and textured. With new batteries, objects are clearer, and colors and textures stand out. The closer you come to your center, the brighter the light of your awareness. The brighter your light, the more you will see. Everything will become more intense as you move inward. You will encounter the same old ego patterning, and you will experience the same sensations in the veils—but the quality of your light, your awareness, changes. That is why the inner experience becomes more intense as you approach your true centers.

Once you have begun processing the veils, light—however dim it may be in the beginning—starts to dawn. It does not dawn though, in the way you expect. In the ego experience, you create a series of ego identities, one layered on top of another. The experience of *me* is a false identity, but an identity nonetheless. As you awaken, you expect a new identity to emerge—a special, spiritual identity—and it probably will … several times. But even as you grow comfortable in this new identity, it too will begin to dissolve. You do not undergo the process of awakening to create a new perfect identity, but to remove the false identities you have assumed, and Existence will not be supporting new identities, no matter how spiritual or holy they are. So—absent a new identity, how will you know the process is working? How will you know that you are indeed awakening?

You will know it by an absence. As the veils dissolve, so do the ego patterning and hot buttons attached to them. Now, when a familiar hot button is pushed, by chance or by intent, you will find that you are no longer plugged into old defensive or offensive patterns. You will notice the absence of pain when someone tries to hurt you—the absence of fear when someone tries to scare you. When this begins to happen, you are on the way home.

By awakening, you are returning to a state of naturalness—a state of *you*. As you awaken, you will begin to feel more and more ordinary, more comfortable in your own body, and more and more like *you*. Labels that you have relied on in the past to define yourself,

As your awakening deepens, you will become increasingly aware of a sense of coming home, of returning to yourself.

start to disappear. Even when you are distracted, looking for some new identity, *you* are appearing. You don't notice what is happening because it feels so natural and ordinary. As your awakening deepens, you will become increasingly aware of a sense of coming home, of returning to yourself. Your thoughts will be along these lines—'I may not know yet who *me* is, but I feel more and more like who I really am—like who I have always been.'

As the veils dissolve, you will begin to slip into your true centers. After processing intense pain sensations, you will find yourself in your Soul center. There you will feel and become pure love. After processing the fear veil you will find yourself in your Spirit center, trusting the world, and tasting pure clear awareness. These states are transitory, as what remains of the veils draws you back into ego darkness. After having experienced the light of *you*, this ego darkness will seem blacker than ever, though it is not. It is merely the contrast between the light of *you* and the darkness of the ego. The experience of slipping into your centers will give you a sense of reward, and will stiffen your resolve to stay the course until you are fully awakened.

As old ego patterns dissolve, you may become dissatisfied with those around you who are not awakening. As you change, you will find it harder to be with them, for they will continue to interact with you only through the old familiar patterns. As you become more real, and desire to connect with something real in them, you will find that maintaining these ego connections will seem increasingly boring, unfulfilling, and even draining.

For their part, it will seem to them that you are becoming increasingly distant and disconnected from them. They may turn strange or hostile towards you, as their own patterns of abandonment are triggered. If you encounter this behavior, you may attempt to do something about it, particularly if your Soul loves the other person. If you try explaining what is happening, they will misinterpret or misunderstand, for unless they too are awakening, they *cannot* understand.

As your awakening deepens, especially after the fear and pain veils are cleared, these people will become more frustrated and perplexed with you. For once Soul is liberated, she will not be connected to anyone's pain again, even that of a loved one. Awakened, Soul knows absolutely the nature of the pain, and she will never again want to connect with it. Even when another that is dear to her wants her to respond with love and attention when it is in pain, she will be unwilling to feed the pain tormenting that other soul—particularly one that she loves. If your Soul does not respond to another's pain the way she *should*, you will see that other person's angry God emerge to blame and punish you. It is the same for Spirit. Once awakened, he will not respond to someone else's fear, as he did in the past. For once clear, Spirit knows the nature of fear, and will not connect to or support another's fear. You will find yourself in detached awareness, as Spirit either attempts to help the other understand the nature of the veil, or else simply waits, detached, until the drama has run its course.

In either case, if the other person is neither aware nor awakening, you will seem to them to be cold, heartless, and insensitive. But by the time this begins to happen, you will be well enough along in the process to value your Soul and Spirit more than the ego judgments directed to you.

As you dissolve the veils, you will notice an increased sensitivity to the thoughts and feelings of others. You are not becoming more sensitive. You are just removing walls of insensitivity that are the veils. When you

As you dissolve the veils, you will notice an increased sensitivity to the thoughts and feelings of others.

are in the pain veil you will feel very sensitive, for you will be in your most sensitive center—Soul. You will notice that the pain veil also feels like a wall. Soul is sensitive to this wall of pain, but insensitive to the world beyond it. If you observe some other Soul lost in the pain veil, you will see that they will not be present to their surroundings. A Soul lost in the pain is no longer in the world—no longer in reality. She is present, sensitive, to the veil, which makes her absent or insensitive to reality—the world around her.

As the pain veil is dissolved, the sensitivity that is Soul begins to feel and interact directly with the environment. As this occurs, she sometimes experiences herself reeling, as though being assaulted by the energy surrounding her. She begins to feel what the rest of the natural world feels in the presence of ego energy—assaulted and drained. The feeling is one of wanting to crawl out of your skin. When this happens, know it is your Soul screaming to remove her from a particular environment. When possible, do so. When impossible, at least acknowledge to Soul that you have heard her. She will understand if it is impossible to remove her immediately. She will be fine. But once she enters the newness of the awakened state, it will take a while for her to get her bearings—to move in and through the ego world with minimal damage.

Awakened from her long experience of *shoulds*, Soul will continue to try to be present to people and situations the way she was taught that she should be. She needs to understand that she has moved beyond the world of *shoulds* and into the world of freedom. In her liberated state, the only *should* for Soul is to be present when it feels good to be present, and to disappear when it feels bad. There is no *doing* to this. It is a simple recognition that if an environment or situation doesn't feel good to be in, she no longer has to remain in it. And with that recognition, she disappears.

If Soul disappears, you will instantly shift centers, moving into either Spirit or God. In either case, since both are masculine and detached, you will automatically disconnect from the energy around you. Over time, this all happens automatically. Soon you will find yourself smoothly shifting to Spirit or God the moment you enter the world. You will move through the world with a quality of detachment. Soul will appear to certain people at certain times, when she will be appreciated, not ravaged or drained. Spirit will protect her by moving forward in consciousness, whenever a situation is uncomfortable or injurious to her. She will no longer play the role of sacrificial lamb to all the angry Gods looking for a convenient receptacle for their toxicity. Her days of being sacrificed to the ego beast are over forever.

As the veils dissolve, the ego chatter being generated by the veils begins to dissolve, and gaps of silence start appearing. Because you are used to focusing on a stream of continuous chatter, these gaps will be hard to discern at first. Initially, you will become aware of them after the fact. You will think, "what just happened?" In other words, you will initially become aware of a gap in the stream of chatter only after the fact. These gaps are pure awareness, places in which there is no object to focus on. Because you identify with your thoughts, when a break in the continuous stream of inner chatter appears, you will likely feel as if you have disappeared. In fact, the exact opposite is happening. You are beginning to appear—aware.

These gaps are very important, for they are the beginning

of silence, peace, and freedom from the constant mindless noise that is the ego experience. The silence in the gaps is initially very delicate, and it is tricky to hold your awareness in the silence without disturbing it with the thought "I'm in the gap". Nonetheless, it is important to recognize the appearance of gaps in the continuous ego chatter, then to become aware of the silence in the gap without disturbing it. You must cultivate an awareness of silence, rather than a thought of silence. Once you are able to be aware *in* the silence of the gap without disturbing it with a thought, then the gap, the silence, will begin to expand. You will begin to experience consciousness as a vast sky with clouds (thoughts) floating by, sometimes quickly, sometimes slowly, sometimes light and airy, sometimes dark and heavy. Sometimes your sky will be clear and silent, sometimes overcast or stormy. But whatever the nature of the clouds, you are becoming more and more identified with the sky, less and less identified with the thoughts floating by.

As your awakening deepens, the silence within will deepen. More and more, thoughts will be there when you need them to cognate experience and to conceptualize. In other words, when you need to think, your mind will be there. When you

After the removal of the pain and fear veils, a space of your own becomes important. You will need a place where your Soul can be alone.

don't need to think, there will be silence. This is the beginning of using your mind, rather than being used by it.

After the removal of the pain and fear veils, a space of your own becomes important. You will need a place where your Soul can be alone. She will need periods where she can relax, whether in silence, in front of the television, or curled up with a book—whatever works for your Soul. What I am trying to describe, is a process of centering, rebalancing and rejuvenation.

Reflect on the times you return home from the office, wanting only to relax and unwind. You are short tempered with your spouse and children, internally screaming *I need time to be alone*. This is your Soul making known her need for time and space in which to center and rejuvenate. After the awakening of both Soul and Spirit, this need becomes more urgent. If you do not pay attention, if you do not

After the Soul and Spirit awakening, one way or another you will learn to take care of your Soul, for the more you care for her, the more you will feel taken care of.

honor and provide for Soul's need, you will find a cranky God emerging to demand it. Of course, if the anger veil has not yet cleared, you will find the emergence of your angry God very effective in clearing away whatever it is disturbing Soul's ability to relax and simply *be*. However, you are then stuck in an angry God, whose presence disallows the very *being-ness* He was trying to enable.

Every situation, like every awakening, is unique. You will somehow provide for time and space for your soul to quietly *be*. You will quickly learn that if you do not nourish and provide Soul's needs, your emotional and mental states will suffer. Remember, Soul is the very root of your growing tree. The strength and stability of the entire tree is dependent on the strength and stability of its roots. After the Soul and Spirit awakening, in one way or another you will learn to take care of your Soul, for the more you care for her, the more you will feel taken care of.

With the removal of the pain and fear veils, very profound changes start to happen within. To understand these changes, you will need to understand the nature of energy. Energy flows. In the ego state it flows into the veils—love energy flows into the pain veil, trust energy flows into the fear veil. In the ego state, you neither love nor trust yourself. You cannot love *self*, for love is not flowing to self, but into a wall separating self from self. You cannot trust *self*, for trust is flowing into a wall separating self from self.

With the removal of these two veils, everything changes. For love, once liberated, has to flow somewhere, and it begins to flow to Spirit. The Spirit self begins to feel loved. For the first time, you really know what it means to love oneself—not ego narcissistic love, but the real thing. For the love which is being generated in your feminine Soul center, is now naturally moving to your masculine Spirit center. In your Soul center you feel love being generated, and in your Spirit center you feel love being received. Once this begins to happen, you will never again enter a relationship a beggar, for once love begins moving within, your Soul and Spirit—your feminine and masculine centers—have entered a love affair.

You will no longer enter external relationships from a place of emptiness or neediness. If you now enter a relationship with someone who has not awakened, you will encounter the subtle, enslaving patterns of ego and ego relationships. But having once tasted freedom, your soul and spirit will not readily exchange it for slavery, however cleverly disguised.

Having liberated Spirit you have also liberated trust, another energy that seeks to flow. After a lifetime of fearing love, of fearing Soul, something new begins to happen. That liberated trust begins to flow to Soul, masculine to feminine. You become aware that you trust yourself as you never have before. Soul, the place where you never felt trusted, becomes the recipient of trust, and you now find that you trust yourself completely. The circuit is complete. Spirit trusts Soul who had never been trusted. Soul loves Spirit, who had longed to be loved. The beautiful twins, isolated and turned against each other by the ego separation, are once again reunited. They begin to merge—masculine into feminine, feminine into masculine— consummating the first alchemical marriage. A sense of unity and wholeness begins to emerge. Everything leading up to the lifting of these two veils is work, but the passage through your dark night of the Soul is now complete.

As these two centers merge and harmonize, you are laying the stable foundation to support the awakening of God. You begin to move from the human dimension of consciousness into the cosmic, the divine. While it seems to suggest a sequential progression—Soul Spirit God—awakening does not

Spirit trusts Soul who had never been trusted. Soul loves Spirit, who had longed to be loved. The beautiful twins, isolated and turned against each other by the ego separation, are once again reunited.

happen in a linear fashion. You will be likely dealing with your God center even while clearing the Soul / Spirit veils, but during the Soul / Spirit passage the focus will be on the pain and fear veils. As these are cleared, the focus moves to God.

Eden to God Consciousness

As you move into the awakening of God, the focus of awareness will shift slowly from Soul / Spirit, to God and His anger. It will seem like a spotlight is being focused on God, a light of increasing intensity. Soul and Spirit, now safe, begin to fade into the background. As they do, you will find yourself more and more often in your God center, heavy and serious. The light playfulness of Spirit will seem less and less present. The tender delicacy of Soul will seem to fade into memory. You will miss them, but trust that they will be there to welcome God as He emerges from His long, dark nightmare. The beautiful children of God, Spirit and Soul, will simply hide until the storm of God's awakening has passed.

Although fragments of the pain and fear veils will continue to percolate into consciousness as you move into your God center, a simple glance will now be sufficient to dissolve them. After the passage through the pain and fear veils is complete, you will be looking forward to a respite from processing, a period of rest. You will probably have time to stabilize in the newness of Eden Consciousness. Nevertheless, however much time existence allots you, it will never be enough, for existence has her own schedule. But God holds the will, and He will not be anxious to surrender it. This is the underlying theme of the passage to God Consciousness ... the surrender of God's will to the flow of existence. True to its nature, anger will constantly distract God. But as the anger veil dissolves, God will become more and more aware that He was basically angry at existence because the whole of existence would not bend to His will. As He awakens, God becomes aware of the lunacy of it all, of 6 billion angry Gods all demanding that existence bend to their individual distorted wills. Even then, anger will continue to battle, to struggle, to control that which is beyond the ability of any individual God to control.

If you have spent lot of time in your angry God center— resentful, angry, and attempting to control everyone around you—you will now begin to see what you are doing. Before the Soul / Spirit awakening, this was almost impossible to do, for you were blinded in all three centers by the veils. After the Soul / Spirit passage, you have two clear centers of consciousness through which you can see again, and whatever you see through them, God also sees. The best way to describe this part of the process is that you begin to see and feel what others have always seen and felt when in the presence of your angry, vengeful God.

After the Soul / Spirit passage, you have two clear centers of consciousness through which you can see again, and whatever you see through them, God also sees.

Not knowing your God and His ego patterning, I cannot predict what He will begin to see, only that He probably won't like what is revealed to Him. God is the place of pride, whether hidden or embraced. When He begins to see how anger transforms Him, feel how ugly anger makes Him, see how mean, self-righteous and arrogant He becomes when controlled by anger, He will not like what He sees. The experience is one of being caught in the anger, while simultaneously standing outside of it, witnessing it. This is the key to the awakening of God, for like previous veils, the key to dissolving the anger veil is to detach from it. However, there is no sensation to focus on, to detach and watch. But with two centers clear, God is able to see what anger has done to His intelligence, creativity and truth. In the seeing, His energy begins to be withdrawn from the anger veil, and the veil begins to dissolve.

At times during the awakening of God, He may feel as if He is battling some beast within, and of course he is—an illusionary beast of His own creation. The Warrior is one of the many masks of God, and it is unlikely that your God will get through this passage without encountering His warrior past. He is also likely to pass through the masks of the Leader, Mentor, or Priest. Whatever masks or identities your God has cultivated over countless lifetimes will in some way be experienced during this passage. Do not become attached to any identities or masks that you encounter. Remain focused on the anger, and the masks will fall away. The goal for God is to leave the divided world of good and evil created by the anger veil, and enter the world of "is-ness", the world of peace. As

The goal for God is to leave the divided world of good and evil created by the anger veil, and enter the world of "is-ness", the world of peace.

the anger veil dissolves, God begins to glimpse peace. As He experiences it, His determination will be renewed to be done with the constant conflict and angst created by the ego anger.

With the dissolving of the anger veil, God comes back to His senses, and everything that preceded His awakening will seem more and more like a dream. Tasting more and more of the clarity and silence of the *now*, God will be anxious to make up for lost time, and to act. Grand ideas and schemes will arise, and He will be anxious to get on with life and do great things in the world. He may initiate projects, only to find them fizzling out, as though existence is not supporting Him. In all likelihood He will be right, and what remains of His anger will tend to be more clearly directed towards the world. If God has not yet realized what has been happening, it will now become apparent—He has been fighting a holy war with existence—with nature—with the Mother. Existence has been responding the way any mother responds to the father's anger—with cold indifference. This indifference will, later on, be revealed as yet another veil—the Mother or Serpent veil. However, during God's awakening, He will not know this. All God will know is that He has done a lot of work waking up, and existence should be rewarding Him with success, riches and abundance. Existence should support His schemes and creativity. But all He receives is this cold indifference.

Perhaps in the past, God has been able to assert His will and overcome all obstacles to achieve success. Now though, He lacks the will to push His plans through to attainment. In dissolving the anger, God has also dissolved His individual will. Suffice it to say, the passage to God Consciousness is not without its frustrations. The powerful creative force that is God, is anxious to "do" things, but God has less and less will to impose upon creation—upon the flow of existence. His internal struggle is between what remains of the ego, struggling to hold on and keep things as they have been, and a peace that beckons Him to relax and let the river carry Him to the sea.

One of the great lessons God must learn as He awakens, is patience. Patience, not indifference, is the message of existence. God will be struggling with the spiritual adage "thy will, not my will, be done". If one were to apply an attribute to existence, it would be flow, not will. Will belongs to God. But because it is the God center now awakening, we perceive what is happening as a struggle of wills—the will of God *vs.* the will (or flow) of existence. God has come far, but the ego in its death throes, will continue to fight and struggle. Nevertheless, at this point the end of ego is only a matter of time. Hence the need for patience.

The ancient journey is coming to its end, but before God can slip into the arms of existence, the ocean of bliss from whence He came, God must first come to a point of stillness. God was born out of the silence and stillness, and to return home, to complete the circle, He must return to that place of stillness. It is not about God becoming inactive, but about God mastering stillness. Only in stillness will He slip back into the ocean. Then the ocean, the whole of existence, will begin to move through God, and He will become active again, even though no longer *doing*. He will no longer be struggling with existence—He will be existence itself.

During this passage to God Consciousness, there will be a deepening feeling of aloneness. Like all states encountered on the journey, this aloneness has always been there. Whatever ego patterning you have to deny or run from, it will now begin to emerge. But like all ego patterns at this stage of the journey, these too will fail. They will fail because you are too awake now, and the distracting patterns are too weak to hide the reality of the moment.

It does not matter what your physical reality is—whether you are physically alone during this passage, or in the midst of family and friends. The feeling will be the same—one of being alone in the universe—and this feeling will deepen during the passage. Fear not—for like everything on the journey, the only absolute is change, and this aloneness too will pass. But it will pass only after God has accepted and relaxed into the aloneness, and the final veil has lifted. For in

At this point He sees that both sides of issues are right, and both are wrong, and to choose is to support the conflict and madness that is destroying everything.

God consciousness, God still *is*, and God can only exist separate from the whole. The aloneness describes a relationship with existence, and God can only feel alone as long as He is separate from existence. With the dissolving of the final veil, God slips into the ocean of consciousness, becomes existence itself, and the aloneness disappears—revealed as simply part of the illusion of separation.

As God awakens, He looks into the world more and

more clearly. Without the anger veil dividing and distorting perception, He begins to see what *is*. No longer forced by anger to take sides in the war of good and evil, He begins to see and hear clearly. What He sees is a world of half-truths and lies, deceit and madness. Those around Him who have not awakened will urge Him, as they always have, to side with their views, their truths in the world of good and evil. But awakened, God will now see the truth of both sides of an issue, and will recognize that the issue (whatever it may be) is not the problem, but rather, the anger fueling it. God will be less and less inclined to take anyone's side in this endless cycle. He will begin living in the middle, no longer supporting or fighting for any side. At this point He sees that both sides of issues are right, and both sides are wrong, and to choose a side is to support the conflict and madness that is destroying everything. More and more, peace beckons to God.

God to Nirvanic Consciousness

While this is all occurring, the final veil begins to appear. This is the Serpent veil, the veil of the Mother. Awareness of this veil does not occur until enough of the anger veil has been dissolved, enough of God is present to see. In the beginning of God's passage everything seems to be coming up anger, and it feels like you have always been in the anger veil. You always have been. All that has changed is that now you are aware of it. The light of awareness, so long distracted, is now focused within. Now there is no avoiding what *is*. As the anger veil dissolves, simply through the growing awareness of God, you will reach a point when He becomes aware of the final veil. He begins to notice a sensation in the chest area, which seems to precede and trigger what has become, at this point, intermittent flare-ups of anger. It is a feeling of irritability, a sensation that can be watched and cleared, just as the Soul and Spirit veils were cleared by detached watching.

It is very difficult to attach a label to this veil, so when I suggest that you watch for the feeling of irritability I am only trying to point to the place where one enters the veil. In identifying the sensation of irritability, God enters the veil. Creation scripture describes this veil thusly: "The Serpent was more subtle than any beast of the field which the lord God had made." The Serpent veil is subtle, mysterious, and beyond accurate description. The door to the veil is the sensation of irritability in the chest area. Once entered, simply watch the sensation whenever it is present. Look for it when you feel the anger appearing. It will move across the breast area, and can move up and down the center of the chest. It is deep, subtle, and at times grueling.

There is a great temptation to stop in God Consciousness, but you must not. You will find it difficult to live in the world until this veil is cleared.

At times it will seem as though you are following a root of discomfort spiraling deep within. As it clears, the sensation will become more focused in the center of the chest. As you clear this veil you will be rewarded with silence, deepening clarity, and waves of bliss. In the East there is a description of consciousness called *samadhi with seed*. Samadhi is God Consciousness, and the seed is this veil—the Serpent or Mother veil—the birthplace of the other veils. There is a great temptation to stop in God Consciousness, but you must not. You will find it difficult to live in the world until this veil is cleared.

You can identify when consciousness is lost in this veil, by some of the mental states that it produces. The most common mental state experienced in the veil will usually follow an episode of anger, when you slip into icy coldness and say to yourself, "I don't care about anything or anyone". Unlike the uncaring states experienced during the Soul passage, which were personal and related to individuals perceived as responsible for Soul's pain, when you are in the Mother / Serpent veil your uncaring states are impersonal. They are universal and universally nihilistic. In the Mother / Serpent veil we become aware of and experience bitterness towards life.

Since you will once again be working a masculine / feminine polarity as you move through the Mother veil, you will go from the heat and passion of God's anger, to the icy death-like grip of the Serpent. Moving more and more into the Mother / Serpent veil, God's passion seems spent. All that remains is a sense of coldness, disinterest in life, and a feeling of death. Before you become alarmed, remember that at this point you will be awake, already in your enlightenment. Be alert, watch the sensation when present, and patiently await your deliverance.

During this passage through the Mother / Serpent veil you

will also notice that you are very sensitive to the energy of others as it moves through their ego veils and is directed at you. Those close to you, particularly those who are near and dear to your Soul will, unless awakened, prove trying. It will seem as if you are picking up their energy—receiving their thoughts. This will make your God cranky. After encounters with these people He will find himself having to watch fear and pain sensations that are not his. He will resent having to clear the toxic energy of others, and yet will feel helpless to protect Himself short of avoiding their company. But this too will prove an imperfect solution, for God will find Himself inundated with pain energy as these people project their hurt feelings upon Him for His absence. This will be followed by the battering energy of their God's anger, blaming your God for abandoning them.

It is not just the negative thoughts and feelings of others that will bedevil God through the Mother passage. Positive thoughts and desires will also become intrusive. God will experience all of it, both positive and negative, as a disturbance to the delicate peace and silence He is seeking to cultivate. At times it will feel to Him as if those near him are robbing him of the fruits of His labors. Although at times He will feel resentment, without the veil of anger He will be unable to blame.

God needs to be vigilant and alert. Though awake, He still has a cosmic address in time and space, an address where the ego projections of others can still reach Him. This will be particularly true of those whose Soul is still linked in love, for that link will provide a direct energy conduit to you. The

Mother / Serpent veil is both that address, and also the screen upon which the thought and image projections of others take form, floating into awareness as one's own. The experience of receiving these projections from others only adds to God's feeling of isolation and aloneness. What is perceived by others as withdrawal from the world, is perceived by the awakened God as being driven out of the world by the madness of others.

The Mother / Serpent veil is a bizarre place on the journey, a place where reality seems more fluid, more dreamlike. Simply continue watching the sensations—subtle, dull, and beyond meaning or labels—and as the veil slowly dissolves and the disturbance from without begins to cease, your consciousness will begin to be permeated with bliss.

12. Sex

This book would be incomplete without touching upon the topic of sex, an issue that has plagued religion and spirituality for so long. The natural world is very sexual and sensual. Some Masters characterize existence as a love affair, and in observing nature you would have to agree. Everywhere you look in nature, there are sexual encounters. Whether it is the exchange of pollen in the plant world, or semen in the animal world, sex is everywhere and it is always happening.

But in the ego experience, nothing is natural or simple. In ego separation it is easy to forget that we are part of this natural sexual world. Sex is truly the last place where we can be natural, the last contact we have with the bliss we knew so long ago. Ironically, this last link we have to the divine, has been condemned by the religions of the world, though I do not believe it has been by deliberate intent. Nonetheless, as a marketing strategy for religions, this condemnation is brilliant. Condemn the last remaining natural link to the divine and create an exclusive monopoly. Tell the world, *If you want the divine you must come through us. There is no other way.* As I said, I do not intend to impart the suggestion of evil intent by religions—after all, they too have suffered from this condemnation, as evidenced by scandals that have plagued various churches over the years. Like the rest of humanity, religions too are crippled and controlled by ego.

It is understandable why sex would be condemned by ego. As ego grew, became sophisticated, and fancied itself civilized, it was not only becoming more separate from nature, but was also looking down at nature with contempt—as though the ego embodied something superior to nature, something separate from, and elevated above it. As we became more lost in the ego, the messages and philosophy it was creating for us made sense.

Sex is the part of the natural world that ego cannot control, and the heart of the ego illusion is the belief that we can control life.

Ego's cruelty and stupidity were attributed to our animal past, a past that was inferior to the superior world of the mind, where ego lived. Sex is a constant reminder to ego that it has not, and cannot, escape the human link to the natural world. The heart of the ego illusion is the belief that we can control life, and sex is the part of the natural world that ego cannot control.

The experience of orgasm, the feeling and bliss, is an ancient echo, a reminder of where we come from. As such, sex is very important to all three centers of consciousness, to all three parts of who we are. In that instant of bliss is the memory of what it felt like to be *one*, before the fall, before the separation of consciousness and its subsequent conflict and suffering. In the East the path of Tantra is just this—to use sex in a conscious, mindful, meditative way as a path to the divine. In the hands of an awakened Tantric master, sex is a very powerful medium of awakening. If you focus on awakening the centers, the Tantra will follow like a shadow.

While awakening, the most important guidance about sex is to just be as natural as you can be with it, though when engaging with partners, be mindful that the bedroom is very crowded. In the world of good and evil, ego has created huge expectations, boundaries, hot buttons, control, violence, and revenge, accompanied by a plethora of laws to regulate and punish the ego's 'crazy' behavior.

In awakening, sex, like everything else in life, becomes transformed. In the ego world, sex is the barometer of love, for while the ego cannot know love, it *can* know sex. This is why to the ego, sex assumes such importance in relationships. Love cannot be touched, measured, stored, controlled, or accumulated. Sex, however, is something physical. Your ego can know if you are getting sex. Ego pays for sex, and deludes itself that it is buying love. Love cannot be bought or known by ego, but sex can. Hence, in the ego world, love is sex.

As Soul awakens, she realizes that sex is not love, and with that realization things naturally change for Soul. She remains open to sex, which is fun and provides an opportunity to connect with another soul and merge in ecstasy. However, Soul will lose interest in partners who provide her with disconnected soulless sex, without love or merging or intimacy. This will not be a denial or repression of sex, but a natural change arising from the growing awareness that sex is an expression of love only when Soul is present When Soul is absent, sex is simply sex. In this age of soul-denial, sex is increasingly just sex. You can enjoy it when it is there and feels right, but do not confuse it with love unless you feel love flowing.

Once Eden consciousness has been attained, sex changes dramatically. The ego obsessions for and against sex arising out of the fear and pain veils, will fade. Soul and Spirit will be left in a much more natural place regarding sex. The fear that held Spirit back, now dissolved, allows Spirit to be more adventurous or playful. The pain imprisoning Soul, now dissolved, allows Soul to connect in deeper ways than she has ever known. However, if a partner is not awake, Spirit's and Soul's newfound freedom will encounter the fear and pain boundaries of the other, and will be disappointed at being unable to explore with that partner, the world of potential now open to Spirit and Soul themselves. To be with a sleeping (i.e. un-awakened) partner is especially difficult for Soul, for her delicate energy, now free and able to flow, is easily thrown off when connecting to another's ego energy. Each time she establishes a rhythm, the flow hits a dam, completely throwing her off.

Once Eden consciousness has been attained, sex changes dramatically. The ego obsessions for and against sex arising out of the fear and pain veils, will fade.

Even before Soul and Spirit are entirely awake, something interesting starts to happen. As the veils dissolve, Soul energy begins to flow to Spirit, Spirit energy to Soul, and you begin to experience flashes of what can only be described as orgasm, but without sex. When masculine and feminine begin to meet inside, little mini-orgasms are experienced. They are not as intense as sexual orgasm, but clearly recognizable as feeling similar. These feelings or sensations occur on and off throughout the Soul / Spirit passage. At times they will be so intense that you will feel washed over with bliss. This is all a natural result of the inner male (Spirit) beginning to merge with the inner female (Soul). It is the re-emergence of the love affair *within*, a love that in ego darkness has, over time, become sour.

With the experience of an awakening Soul and Spirit, a new sense of self is being born. Your Soul, no longer starved for love, no longer a beggar, recognizing the difference between love and sex, is no longer so easily manipulated or willing to settle for loveless relationships. Besides, she discovers that some of the intermittent flashes of bliss which she experiences spontaneously are more satisfying that a lot of the sex she has had. Spirit, awake, has similar experiences. As he merges more and more with Soul, his growing respect and admiration for her makes him less likely to expose her to energy that is toxic, simply for sex. It is one of those 'guy things', in the best sense of the phrase.

Sex changes with the Soul / Spirit passage, in different ways for each individual. The commonality is that sex will begin to feel more natural, less encumbered with emotional baggage. It may not look the way experts say it should, but to you it will begin to feel more natural, more easy, more like how it should be for you.

Orgasms, alone or with a partner, will begin changing. With the Soul / Spirit awakening and the removal of major energy blocks of pain and fear, orgasmic feeling begins to move upwards. This will happen over time, as the energy once confined by the veils, begins to move over ancient pathways in the physical body, opening up what was for so long blocked and unused. No longer confined to the genital area, the stomach area and above will begin to pulsate in ecstasy. The orgasmic feeling will expand up to the heart, but will neither reach that high nor beyond, until you have cleared the God and Mother veils. The Mother veil runs across the chest, and until it is cleared, orgasm cannot spread upwards.

As the father and mother veils dissolve, the experience of orgasm moves upwards, through the heart area and to the crown (the head), the whole body pulsating with ecstasy. Sexual orgasms are no longer confined to one area of the body, and even the sense of a center from which the orgasm is spreading outwards, begins to disappear. However, the orgasm still seems to have a boundary—the body. As the mother veil dissolves, the final separation from existence disappears, and the experience of sexual orgasm subtly changes. Now there is no center and no boundary. The experience becomes one of the whole of existence pulsating in ecstasy, with no beginning and no end.

What began with the Soul / Spirit awakening (uncaused waves of bliss) becomes, with the awakening of God, more intense, as the father masculine begins merging once again with the mother feminine. This is the beginning of Nirvanic consciousness. What starts as waves of bliss, as energies begin merging and resuming their ancient dance, begins to permeate consciousness, producing a feeling of well-being similar to orgasm. Unlike orgasm, which is hot and intense, this bliss is cool and subtle.

After this point, you can move to celibacy or not. Some of you may ask, *"Why go through the trouble for something I already have?"* Celibate or not, sex has returned to its natural state. If sex disappears, the event will seem as natural as a leaf falling from a tree in autumn. Nothing will feel forced, repressed, or denied. From the Soul / Spirit awakening onward, having sex with a partner who is un-awakened becomes increasingly difficult.

From the Soul / Spirit awakening onward, having sex with a partner who is un-awakened becomes increasingly difficult.

You will continuously run into your partner's roadblocks, boundaries, and hidden minefield of hot buttons. At this point your own energy, though more integrated, is also more delicate. In intimate settings like a bedroom, where an un-awakened partner's energy is all over the place, it will be impossible to feel balanced, focused and *present* to the moment. Remember— when you are bedding down with someone who is 'asleep', you are not engaging with one person, but with three—Soul, Spirit and God—each one encumbered with emotional baggage, boundaries and hot buttons.

The holy wars have invaded the bedroom with a vengeance, wreaking havoc as only fallen Gods can do. Understand that the unspoken, seductive *yes* to sex is Soul in her unconditional *yes*. The carved in stone *no* is the angry, vengeful God. Be aware, this God is basically anti-feminine. In men, He is the place of violence against women, for He resents needing woman to fulfill His carnal desires. In woman, He is the part that wants to punish men for eons of repression. So a word of warning—

if your partner's God shows signs of violence or irrational
retribution, leave him or her. For until God is awake, there is
no limit to His madness or revenge. Your Soul will recognize
the danger. Listen to her.

Ocean of Consciousness

The Mother Goddess

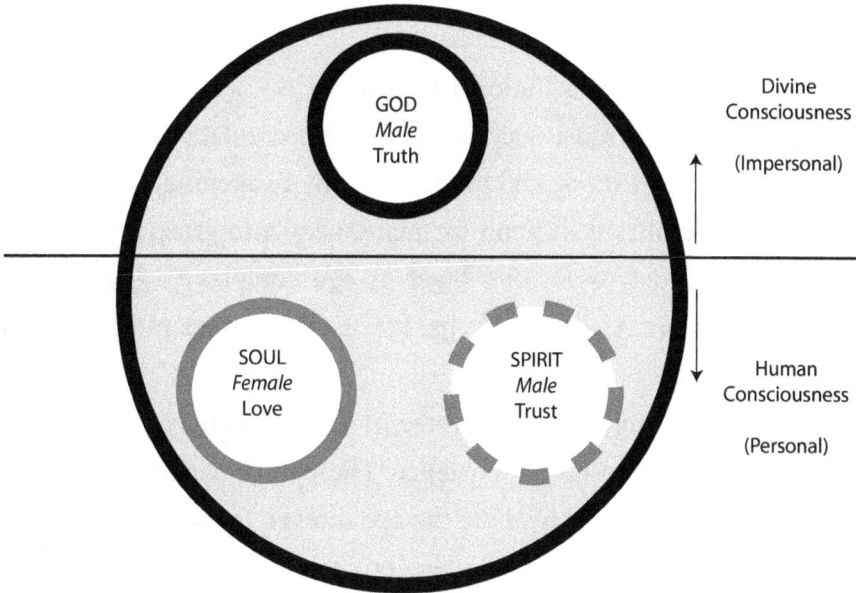

GOD
Male
Truth

SOUL
Female
Love

SPIRIT
Male
Trust

Divine
Consciousness

(Impersonal)

Human
Consciousness

(Personal)

The VEILS

........The GOD center is surrounded by a veil of **anger**

........The SOUL center is surrounded by a veil of **pain**

........The SPIRIT center is surrounded by a veil of **fear**

........The THREE CENTERS are surrounded by the **serpent veil**

Centers of Consciousness

I have used this illustration for years in my teaching, for it is the simplest, most succinct visual representation both of human consciousness, and the teaching of awakening. Its very simplicity makes it difficult for many people to grasp as they study it through layer after layer of ego complexity, beliefs, and confusion. As one awakens, life itself becomes more and more simple.

At your center there are three of you, seemingly adrift in an uncaring, meaningless existence. These three parts each feel incomplete, and search where the ego directs, for relationships with other beings that hold the promise of completion, of wholeness.

The relationships that exist within, are mirrored without. For instance, if the inner God condemns, blames and judges Soul for being lazy, a hopeless dreamer, weak, helpless and needy, then that inner God, encountering another Soul, will judge that Soul in similar ways. Soul herself, accustomed

Until the veils are cleared, whatever the dysfunctional ego relationships patterned within, will continuously be encountered without.

to receiving these judgments within, will expect and receive, these same judgments from the Gods she encounters without. Same with Spirit. If the inner God condemns the inner Spirit for not being serious enough, for being a failure, a coward, or for not working hard enough, these same judgments will be expected and received whenever Spirit encounters Gods without. Until the veils are cleared, whatever the dysfunctional ego relationships patterned within, will continuously be encountered without.

In each center you will feel incomplete. In each center you will be seeking outside that which you sense will make you whole again. Spirit is seeking outside for a loving playmate (Soul), and a protecting, mentoring father (God). Soul is seeking outside for a trusting, intimate companion (Spirit) to care for, nurture and love. She is also seeking a strong protective father (God) to take care of her. God is seeking a son (Spirit) to mentor and teach, someone from whom to receive admiration and respect. He is also seeking a helpless daughter (Soul) to be the protective guardian of.

This is why we compartmentalize our friends in the world. Some people are the friends of God—those who are serious. Notice when you entertain, how you include some friends and exclude others. If God is socializing, he tends to disdain the lightness and frivolity of Spirit's friends, as well as the spacey helplessness of Soul's companions. Just as your Soul and Spirit will tend to exclude God's friends when socializing, knowing that to include that heavy, serious energy will dampen the party, replacing fun with serious discussion at best, arguments at worst.

Each part also has a distorted relationship with existence— each seeing existence through an uncaring veil of indifference (the Mother / Serpent veil), and mis-interpreting the veil as existence. Existence is not indifferent. The Mother / Serpent veil is indifference itself. When your consciousness is caught in this veil and you feel as though you do not care about anything or anyone, you are experiencing the truth of the veil, not the truth of existence.

Each center is a lens through which a fragmented consciousness looks into the world. What it sees is determined by which part is looking, as well as the distortion produced by the lens (veil) itself. As long as the veils exist, you are not seeing reality. You are instead seeing the ego distortions, or projections onto reality. As the veils lift, you begin to see reality. With the lifting

To search for the meaning of life requires that you become separate from life.

of the pain / fear veils, you begin to see your personal reality more clearly. Your small human universe begins to come into focus. You begin to understand and bring into balance your human desires, needs and relationships. But you will lack the ability to see the larger picture clearly—to grasp your place in the universe—your relationship with existence. That comes with the awakening of God, and the dissolving of the Mother / Serpent veil—after which you become existence itself. You will not necessarily understand 'the meaning of it all', for there is no meaning to understand. Having transcended all duality, you will be totally in the *now*, where there is no meaning—only life, experience, and flow. To search for the meaning of life requires that you become separate from life.

As the veils lift, the fragmented parts begin to merge back into one consciousness. First, Soul and Spirit merge into Soul-Spirit consciousness—into one innocence—one that is both tender, loving, and connected, and playful and adventurous. Soul and Spirit are where you are human, and you must first be human before you can be divine. The human plane is a very small, very personal universe. You are taught that you should care about the suffering of the world (Soul), and that you should be interested and engaged in bettering the world (Spirit). But these *shoulds* only serve the ego veils, causing guilt in Soul, and failure in Spirit. All Soul and Spirit really care about are those near and dear to them, and all caring for beings not immediately known at this human level is simply ego pretense.

It is not until you begin awakening God will there be genuine interest in a larger universe. God used to be the steward of the earth, before ego darkness began to blind and control Him. Awakened, with no prodding from ego's *shoulds*, God naturally becomes more concerned with the whole—more aware of the thoughtless damage unconsciously being done to the earth in everyday life. While watching over the personal aspect of life (Soul and Spirit), God increasingly becomes more impersonal in seeing and interacting with a larger universe. With the dissolving of the anger veil, He slips out of the world of good and evil, no longer fighting for good or perpetrating evil. More and more He becomes an impersonal observer of the ego madness of the world of good and evil. He becomes more and more harmless.

With God's awakening, and the awareness of Soul and Spirit that He has returned to His senses, Soul's love once again begins to flow to God. She realizes that He is once again taking care of her, and she is drawn towards His increasing light. Spirit realizes he has been trusting the Gods of others, when the one God who deserves his trust and respect, is the God within. And so, Spirit and Soul begin to merge back into God.

As Soul's love permeates God, His cold hardness begins to soften, and warmth and compassion begin emerging. As Spirit's trust merges Spirit back into God, God once again begins to be just and fair, His seriousness mellowed by Spirit's playfulness. This allows God to once again enjoy life—to enjoy His creation. No more separate or conflicted, He is once again the creative, good and blessing God who entered the garden.

Further splitting or differentiation of Energy Centers into what we know as Archetypes. Also Gods and Goddesses of ancient Greek and Roman religions.

God of Creation
Before the Fall

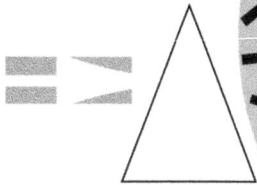

Garden of Eden
Splitting of God into 3 parts

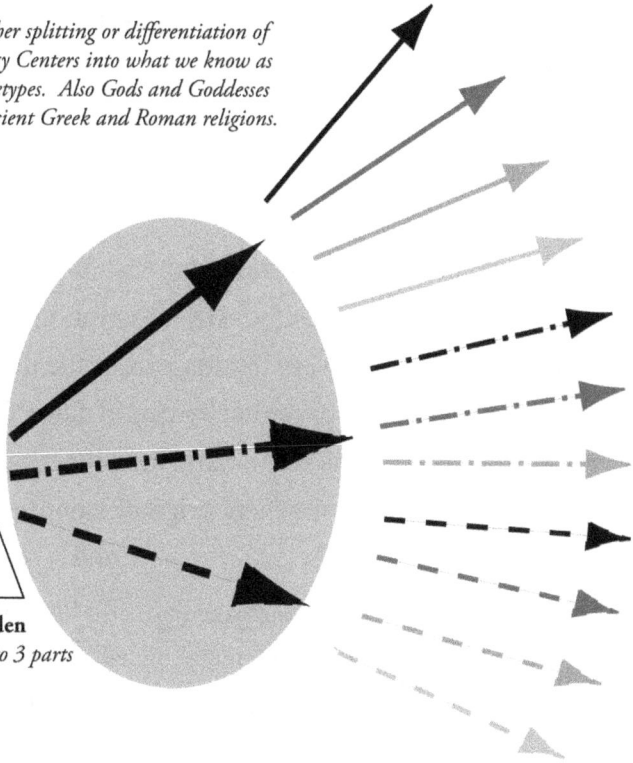

Legend:

White light enters the prism, where it is broken into three primary colors representing the three Centers of Consciousness:

Red is God;
Yellow is Spirit;
Blue is Soul.

The Centers of Consciousness are surrounded by the gray of Veils:

- *God is surrounded by the Veil of Anger;*
- *Spirit is surrounded by the Veil of Fear;*
- *Soul is surrounded by the Veil of Pain.*

The three Centers of Consciousness are further divided into myriad Archetypes.

The Prism Diagram

This book is intended to show the way home, a map to guide seekers through an illusion. Any description of the nature of this illusion is, by its very nature, part of the illusion.

I use the metaphor of the Garden of Eden for a number of reasons. The tale exists very deep in the collective consciousness of all mankind, as do the three original identities—Soul, Spirit and God. If this metaphor is heard and understood in even one of the centers of consciousness, it will be like a beacon being once again lit, a light that will guide the seeker home. Therefore, for those of you who may have difficulty understanding the concepts of split consciousness in terms the Garden metaphor, perhaps using a metaphor about light will be helpful.

Light is the most ancient and enduring metaphor of consciousness and spirituality, and the diagram is a way to illuminate the same tale, the same splitting of consciousness, using an analogy of how light is split when it passes through a prism.

Light is the most ancient and enduring metaphor of consciousness and spirituality, and the diagram is a way to illuminate the same tale, the same splitting of consciousness, using an analogy of how light is split when it passes through a prism.

Out of darkness, out of the void, from the great mother of everything, comes light—the birth of God. When a holy or 'realized' being is depicted in paintings, there is a halo around the head, sometimes around the entire body. This halo is white, indicating a state of consciousness where light is in its original one-ness. Someone who is able to see 'auras' around the human body, is seeing through the filter of their own Soul the subtler levels of reality that permeate and underlie the physical reality with which we are all familiar. What these individuals are seeing is the fragmented light that emerges from the prism in the illustration. If such an individual looks at someone who has been *awakened*, they are looking at someone who has moved backwards through the prism. In such a case, they would see only white light—light in its unity state.

In this illustration, the pure light entering the prism corresponds to the God who entered the Garden. The God is in unity consciousness, not yet split into three—the God before the events of the Fall. The prism is the Garden of Eden, the place where God becomes divided into three parts. Each of the three parts—Soul, Spirit and God—is a component of one unified God. White light enters the prism (God enters the Garden) and splits into three primary colors (Soul, Spirit and God).

The color red represents God after the Fall. From time immemorial, He has been associated with fire. When your inner God explodes with rage, does it not feel fiery—volcanic? The sun, which has been worshipped throughout the ages as a God, is also fiery. Yellow represents Spirit after the Fall. Yellow has a lightness, a quickness that corresponds to Spirit's energy.

Blue, of course, represents Soul after the Fall—moody, deep, dark, and mysterious.

In the same way that all other colors are derived from the interaction of the three primary colors, the many human archetypes are derived from the interactions of Soul, Spirit and God. The ancient Gods and Goddesses of Greece and Rome are nothing but external representations of these archetypal expressions of the essential trinity within.

You must begin your journey home from the rainbow of colors, the multiple archetypes produced by the splitting of light, the ego distortion of consciousness, and return to the center, to the white light. You will do this by passing through the primary colors—the three centers of consciousness—of the original split.

The process of *Awakening* begins at the level of Soul, Spirit and God. Beginning there, I will direct your awareness to the prism in the illustration, the place where white light was split into three colors. By liberating your centers of consciousness from their veils of separation, you will be able to pass back through the prism to the light that emerged from the void—to God.

All that remains is the final step, where God's light disappears back into the ocean of consciousness from which it originally came.

Conclusion

The West has created the most complex ego structure the world has ever known. Its complexity has produced intense feelings of alienation, separation and insensitivity to the world around us—the world of which we are an integral part. Through this ego structure and its division of ourselves and the world into good and evil, we have created great good and equally great evil. The more complex the ego structure, the more inherently unstable it becomes. The society we create through this ego naturally shares these characteristics of increasing complexity and instability—a fact not unknown to terrorists seeking to destroy the West. Our very complexity is our greatest weakness, individually and collectively. We are vulnerable to pressures and stresses, and just as we are prone to individual meltdowns within the ego structure, so too the society we have created through it.

We are in the endgame, and God—the only hope we have at this point—is distracted in the ancient blame game perpetrated by His anger. He needs to realize that the blame game has not healed Soul's pain nor made Spirit safe. The blame, with its attendant conflict and warfare, has never solved personal or global problems. As addictive and compelling as it is to God, the blame game does not work. It has never produced the results that anger claims it will, nor will it ever fulfill its promise of righting wrongs, healing hurts, or creating safety.

But God, possessed and controlled by His ancient advisor cannot see the futility of it all. While He is distracted by anger, precious time slips through His fingers, and we edge closer to the abyss.

I call on God in each one of you to come to His senses. We are the sleeping Gods unconsciously destroying life, and only by choosing to awaken, to become conscious, can we save it. The future is in our hands.

www.ingramcontent.com/pod-product-compliance
Lightning Source LLC
Chambersburg PA
CBHW021108090426
42738CB00006B/553